UNDERSTANDING
A N D
PREVENTING
W O R K P L A C E
RETALIATION

Thompson Publishing Group®
1725 K Street, N.W., Suite 700
Washington, D.C. 20006
202-872-4000 (Editorial Offices)
1-800-677-3789 (Customer Service)

Understanding and Preventing
Workplace Retaliation

Patricia A. Wise   *Author*
Rosemarie Lally   *Copy Editor*
Jerry Kline   *Editor*
Don Montuori   *Assoc. Development Director*
Kathleen Dunten   *Editorial Director*
Roberta Weisberg   *Production Specialist*
Kevin Cuddihy   *Proofreader*
Ellen Hamilton   *Graphic Artist*

Price: $85.00. Discounts available for quantity purchases. Copies of this book can be obtained from:

Thompson Publishing Group, Inc.
P.O. Box 26185
Tampa, FL 33623-6185
(800) 677-3789
www.thompson.com

"This publication is designed to provide accurate and authoritative information in regard to the subject matter covered. It is sold with the understanding that the publisher is not engaged in rendering legal, accounting or other professional service. If legal advice or other expert assistance is required, the services of a competent professional person should be sought." —

From a Declaration of Principles jointly adopted by a Committee of the American Bar Association and a Committee of Publishers and Associations.

Printed in the United States of America
ISBN 1-930872-00-3

▶ Table of Contents

Chapter 4: Preventing Retaliation Claims

Appendix A: Federal Discrimination Laws, Retaliation Provisions

Appendix B: EEOC Guidance

Appendix C: Supreme Court Decision

Appendix D: Sample Documents

▶ Acknowledgments

About the Author . . .

Ms. Patricia A. Wise is a co-founder of the law firm of Wise & Dorner, Ltd., and the founder of Wise People Management, Inc., a human resources consulting firm. Her practice includes all areas of employment law, including discrimination, harassment, non-competition agreements and preventive law. She is an adjunct professor at the University of Toledo College of Law. She holds an undergraduate degree from Bowling Green State University, a juris doctor from the University of Toledo, and a degree from the Stonier Graduate School of Banking at the University of Delaware.

Acknowledgments

Ms. Wise gratefully acknowledges the diligence and enthusiasm of Tracy Hundsrucker in preparing copy, the able and dedicated legal assistance of Dawn Christen and Dawn Wenk, and the constant support, friendship and humor of her law partner, Renisa Dorner. She also extends special thanks to her husband, David, and children, Hannah and Mackenzie.

▶ Chapter 1: Defining Retaliation in the Workplace

What Is Retaliation?

All employers know or should know that they can't discriminate against employees or job applicants on the basis of race, sex, religion, national origin, age or disabilities. Many employers, however, may be completely unaware of one of the biggest risks they face in the area of potential employment discrimination complaints — retaliation.

Retaliation occurs when an employer illegally strikes back at or seeks revenge on an employee or applicant who has complained of discrimination or some other allegedly unlawful act by the employer.

Most employers don't realize the extent of their potential liability for actions taken against employees or job applicants in retaliation for their complaining of discriminatory practices. In recent years, federal laws prohibiting retaliation have established an expansive array of offenses and created entirely new groups of plaintiffs. In addition, many lawyers are relying on 1998 guidance issued by the Equal Employment Opportunity Commission (EEOC) to argue that nearly any adverse action by a supervisor or co-worker, including giving a negative job reference or even excluding the worker from lunch meetings, can support a retaliation claim.

Increasingly, workers who participate in employment discrimination claims and other employment complaints are suing their employers for retaliation. In fact, illegal retaliation is one of the fastest developing and most far-reaching causes of action against employers today. It is now the third most frequent type of discrimination complaint lodged by employees with the EEOC. The EEOC recently reported that retaliation claims filed with the agency jumped from about 7,900 in 1991 to nearly 20,000 in 1999. These claims generally are easier to prove and result in larger damage awards than other discrimination claims, experts say. Retaliation claims are extremely difficult to prevent and even more difficult to defend against. In fact, some well-established, highly regarded methods of addressing discrimination may actually increase potential liability for illegal retaliation.

Unfortunately, broad pronouncements concerning liability leave employers with little guidance in preventing claims due to the fact-specific nature of retaliation cases.

This book is designed to assist employers in bridging that gap by addressing the myriad issues involved in this developing area of the law and providing practical guidance to help employers avoid liability.

Where Did this 'New' Liability Come From?

Actually, potential employer liability for illegal retaliation has existed for some time. It has only recently been recognized as a significant threat to employers, however, as these types of claims have become more common.

Current events have focused a spotlight on retaliation claims, much as the sexual harassment allegations brought by Anita Hill against U.S. Supreme Court nominee Clarence Thomas in 1991 raised public awareness of sexual harassment.

For instance, Internal Revenue Service (IRS) employees testified before the Senate Finance Committee in 1997 and 1998 about taxpayer abuse and agency improprieties. Employees testified behind a screen to conceal their identities from IRS officials, stating that they feared retaliation. Only one IRS agent testified without hiding her identity. Many agents called investigators from pay phones, fearing phone taps or traces of their office and home phones.[1]

As it turned out, their fears were justified. Despite the fact that Sen. William Roth (R-Del.) asked all senior IRS managers to guarantee that there would be no retaliation against IRS employees who testified, he heard from several that they were hounded by their supervisors. One employee, who had always had superior performance ratings, began receiving nothing but failing grades after giving her testimony. Her co-workers were actually warned by their manager to side with the IRS against her if they "[knew] what's good" for them.[2] Since that time, a number of the "whistleblowers" have received damage awards from the courts and, in some cases, promotions to rectify the retaliation they suffered from the agency.

Another egregious example of retaliation surfaced in 1995 in connection with the tobacco industry. Jeffrey Wigand, who had been the research director for Brown & Williamson (B&W) until he was fired in 1993 under disputed circumstances, taped an interview with CBS News' television program "60 Minutes" in 1995. In the interview, which didn't air until 1996, he discussed the company's knowledge of the addictive nature and health effects of nicotine. He also was a star witness in the lawsuit filed by Mississippi against the tobacco industry, alleging that B&W's chief executive had opposed work on safer cigarettes to avoid the possibility of legal liability relating to conventional cigarettes. His former employer sued him in late 1995, accusing him of breaching two confidentiality agreements and of providing stolen documents to *The Washington Post* and *The Wall Street Journal* concerning B&W's interest in a nicotine patch manufacturer.

During the course of litigation, B&W hired lawyers and private investigators to build a 500-page dossier on Wigand, which his former employer then used in its attempts to undermine his credibility and cast him as "a master of deceit," in the words of B&W's counsel. His experience was recently recounted in the film, "The Insider." These recent developments and others have made everyone more aware of this area of employment law.

Some employers may be surprised to learn of the vast scope of this potential area of liability, especially since they may have received little in the way of warning or advance notice about retaliation liability. Recent federal legislation expanding employee rights in the workplace — as well as potential employer liability — has been widely discussed well in advance of its application. For example, employers are quite familiar with the increased rights of plaintiffs under the Civil Rights Act of 1991, increased protection for people with disabilities under the Americans with Disabilities Act, and mandated leave policies under the Family and Medical Leave Act. In contrast, potential liability for illegal retaliation

---

[1] William V. Roth and Bill Nixon, *The Power to Destroy*, pp. 41-60 (1999).
   The testimony did, in fact, lead to significant changes at the Internal Revenue Service, including the appointment of a new tax commissioner and more independent oversight of the agency. In addition, Congress enacted the Internal Revenue Service Restructuring and Reform Act of 1998 to further address agency problems.

[2] *Id.*, pp. 214-215.

by employers under these and other laws is a more insidious threat, seeming to spring up virtually overnight.

The Enforcement Role of the EEOC

The EEOC is the federal agency responsible for enforcing all federal statutes prohibiting employment discrimination. The commission is empowered to sue employers that violate these laws.

The EEOC also issues guidance based on its interpretation of federal statutes. Although this guidance doesn't carry the force of law, the U.S. Supreme Court has said such guidance is entitled to great deference when it supports the views of the Court or Congress.

According to the EEOC, non-discrimination laws are only effective if individuals are able to oppose employment practices that they reasonably believe are unlawful, without fear of retaliation. The EEOC states that claimants must be free to pursue claims of discrimination or of improper payment of compensation, and to expose workplace wrongdoing.[3] If retaliation is not prohibited, many individuals will be deterred from opposing unlawful practices or pursuing these claims for fear of losing their jobs, according to the commission.

Discrimination Laws and Retaliation

A wide variety of discrimination laws prohibit employers from retaliating against employees or former employees who engage in protected activities. These laws include Title VII of the Civil Rights Act of 1964, the Age Discrimination in Employment Act (ADEA), the Americans with Disabilities Act (ADA), the Fair Labor Standards Act (FLSA), the Equal Pay Act (EPA), the Occupational Safety and Health Act (OSHA), state anti-discrimination statutes, and workers' compensation statutes.

Title VII of the Civil Rights Act of 1964 states that it is unlawful "for an employer to discriminate against any of his employees or applicants for employment" who have either availed themselves of Title VII's protections or assisted others in doing so.[4]

Similarly, the ADEA provides that it is unlawful for an employer to discriminate against employees or applicants who have "opposed any practice" of age discrimination or who have "made a charge, testified, assisted, or participated in any manner in an investigation, proceeding, or litigation" regarding age discrimination.[5]

The ADA prohibits discrimination against those who oppose any act of disability discrimination or who participate in any "investigation, proceeding or litigation" of a disability discrimination claim. The ADA further provides that it is unlawful for any person:

> to coerce, intimidate, threaten, or interfere with any individual in the exercise or enjoyment of, or on account of his or her having exercised or enjoyed, or on account of his or her having aided or encouraged any other individual in the exercise or enjoyment of, any right granted or protected by this chapter.[6]

The FLSA protects from retaliation employees who file complaints alleging FLSA violations or who participate in FLSA proceedings initiated by themselves or others. Since 1985, the

---

[3] EEOC Compliance Manual, §8-I(A) and EEOC Notice No. 915.002, III(A)(April 10, 1997)(See Appendix B).

[4] §704(a) of Title VII of the Civil Rights Act of 1964, 42 U.S.C. §2000e-3(a), as amended.

[5] §4 of the Age Discrimination in Employment Act, 29 U.S.C. §623(d).

[6] §§503(a) and (b) of the Americans with Disabilities Act of 1990, 42 U.S.C. §§12203(a) and (b).

FLSA, including its retaliation provisions, has applied to state and local governments. Section 15(a)(3) of the FLSA makes it unlawful for any person:

> to discharge or in any other manner discriminate against any employee because such employee has filed any complaint or instituted or caused to be instituted any proceeding under or related to this [act], or has testified or is about to testify in any such proceeding, or has served or is about to serve on an industry committee.[7]

The Equal Pay Act (EPA) prohibits discrimination "against any employee because such employee has filed any complaint or instituted or caused to be instituted any proceeding . . . or has testified or is about to testify in any such proceeding" regarding wage and hour claims.[8] The EPA does not contain a specific "opposition clause" making it unlawful for an employer to discriminate against employees who have opposed a discriminatory practice, but courts have recognized an implied protection for retaliation based on opposition practices. (The difference between participation and opposition, two kinds of protected activity, is discussed in Chapter 2 of this book.)

OSHA, a statute designed to provide safe workplaces for employees, also prohibits retaliation against employees for testifying in Occupational Safety and Health Administration proceedings or for exercising in any way their rights under the act.[9]

An employer also is prohibited by various federal laws from retaliating against an employee who files a complaint with the Environmental Protection Agency, who participates in National Labor Relations Board cases, or who exercises or attempts to exercise the employee's rights under the Family and Medical Leave Act or the Employee Retirement Income Security Act.

Retaliation claims can also arise under state law when an employer retaliates against employees for filing workers' compensation claims, reporting state wage and hour law violations, complaining about safety or any other workplace issues, participating in union activities, or "whistleblowing." Whistleblowing is reporting an employer's suspected unlawful behavior to the appropriate authorities (in other words, "blowing the whistle"). These retaliation claims are governed by state law.

Damages Available for Retaliatory Conduct

Both compensatory and punitive damages are available to most plaintiffs who file successful retaliation claims, although plaintiffs with valid FLSA and EPA claims may receive only compensatory and liquidated (or double back-pay) damages. Some federal statutes, including the FLSA and EPA, also permit plaintiff employees to recover attorney's fees. In addition, courts hearing certain retaliation disputes may be authorized to award prejudgment interest on unpaid back wages, court costs and witness fees.

Compensatory damages are payments for actual injuries or economic losses suffered by a plaintiff. Compensatory damages provide compensation to victims. Punitive damages, which are not based on any actual injury or loss, are designed to "punish" offenders and to deter future wrongful conduct. They are awarded in addition to compensatory damages. Typically, punitive damages are awarded when retaliation is undertaken with malice or with

---

[7] §15(a)(3) of the Fair Labor Standards Act, 29 U.S.C. §215(a)(3).

[8] Equal Pay Act of 1963, 29 U.S.C. §206(d).

[9] §11(c) of the Occupational Safety and Health Act, 29 U.S.C. §660(c)(1).

Common Legal Terms Defined

(pertaining to employment discrimination)

Compensatory damages: Payment to compensate a victim of employment discrimination for pain and suffering, mental anguish, loss of enjoyment of life and other non-monetary injuries.

Equitable relief: Relief designed to place plaintiffs in the position they would have been in if the harassment had not occurred. Equitable relief includes back pay, interest on back pay and other relief afforded by Title VII, such as reinstatement.

Injunctive relief: A court-ordered remedy requiring that certain activities stop; e.g., an order that an organization refrain from discriminating in the future.

Intentional discrimination: Knowing or purposeful discrimination against an individual as differentiated from an employment practice that appears to be neutral but has an adverse and unlawful impact on a protected group.

Punitive damages: The money employers are ordered to pay to punish them for harassing workers or allowing others to commit harassment. The awards, which are paid to victims of harassment, also are designed to deter future harassment by the defendants and others.

Strict liability: The automatic imposition of liability, regardless of extenuating circumstances, intent or knowledge.

reckless disregard for an employee's legally protected rights.

The total amount of compensatory and punitive damages that each successful plaintiff may recover under Title VII of the Civil Rights Act and the ADA is subject to statutory limits. Compensatory and punitive damages awarded under the ADEA are not capped, nor are compensatory and liquidated damages awarded under the FLSA and EPA. Interestingly, plaintiffs can sometimes obtain greater damage awards by bringing their retaliation claims under state law than federal because the maximum caps often are higher under state laws.

How Much Does Retaliation Cost?

Retaliation claims can be particularly expensive for employers. A 1999 study of retaliation lawsuits decided over the previous six years found that plaintiffs had a 57 percent chance of receiving a favorable jury verdict. Of plaintiffs who received money damages, the median compensatory damage award was $121,547.[10]

In one recent case, a female employee brought a claim of sexual harassment against a supervisor who was fired but later rehired. After the supervisor was rehired, the plaintiff claimed he ignored her, excluded her from meetings and constantly changed her job assignments. An Iowa jury agreed and awarded her $80.2 million, later reduced to $800,000 due to state statutory caps on damages.[11] Similar allegations in Alaska, where a plaintiff actually lost her job, resulted in an original verdict of $3.78 million, which was later reduced to $500,000, the maximum punitive damages allowable under applicable state law.[12]

Valid whistleblowing retaliation cases have resulted in large jury verdicts. For example, a grocery store supervisor was awarded over $1.03 million in damages in a California whistleblowing retaliation suit. He had reported theft and fraud, as well as sanitation and health problems. As a result of his complaints, other grocery store officers were terminated. He was then terminated in what the employer said was a legitimate reorganization. The

---

[10] Jury Verdict Research, 1999 LRP Publications, Vol. 1, Iss. 1 (April 1999).
[11] *Channon v. United Parcel Service*, No. 66303 (Iowa Dist. Ct. Feb. 12, 1998).
[12] *Kotowski v. Norcon Inc.*, No 3AN-90-1121 (Alaska Super. Ct. Oct. 25, 1993).

jury disagreed.[13] Clearly, this is an area where plaintiffs can win sizable damages against employers.

Supreme Court Expands Anti-Retaliation Protections

The U.S. Supreme Court's 1997 decision in *Robinson v. Shell Oil Company*[14] further heightened the importance and prominence of anti-retaliation protections by expanding their scope. In *Robinson*, the Court unanimously held that Title VII of the Civil Rights Act prohibits retaliation against current *and* former employees for participating in any Title VII proceeding, or for opposing any act made unlawful by Title VII. The Court's decision ended a longstanding disagreement among lower courts as to whether Title VII's protections extended to former as well as current employees.

This decision arose from a suit brought by Charles T. Robinson, Sr., a Shell Oil employee who was fired in 1991. Robinson subsequently filed a charge of race discrimination with the EEOC, contesting his discharge. While that charge was pending, Robinson applied for a job with another company, which contacted Shell Oil for an employment reference. Robinson, claiming that Shell Oil gave him a negative reference in retaliation for his having filed an EEOC claim against it, then sued his former employer under Title VII for retaliation.

The district court dismissed his claim, holding that the retaliation provision of Title VII did not apply to former employees. The 4th U.S. Circuit Court of Appeals affirmed the lower court's holding, stating that former employees may not bring suit under Title VII for retaliation that occurs after termination of their employment. The Supreme Court, however, reinstated his claim, holding that retaliation claims based on post-employment actions could be brought by former employees.

In its opinion, the Court expressed agreement with the arguments advanced by the EEOC in an amicus curiae — or "friend of the court" — brief it had filed on behalf of Robinson.[15] The EEOC argued that Title VII's use of the term "employees" must be construed to include former employees because to fail to do so would effectively vitiate much of the protection provided by the statute.

Justice Thomas, citing the EEOC's reasoning with approval, wrote that exclusion of former employees from the protections of Title VII would undermine the statute's effectiveness "by allowing the threat of post-employment retaliation to deter victims of discrimination from complaining to the EEOC, and would provide a perverse incentive for employers to fire employees who might bring Title VII claims." The Court found it was necessary to extend the retaliation provisions of Title VII to cover former employees as well as current employees to provide the protection intended by Congress in enacting the law.

EEOC's Response to the Problem of Retaliation

Bolstered by the Supreme Court's decision in *Robinson*, the EEOC in 1998 issued policy guidance on retaliation. The policy guidance explains what constitutes a claim of illegal retaliation and provides guidance to employers on their obligations under federal statutory retaliation provisions.

---

[13] *Payne v. Certified Grocers of Calif.*, No. BC 153411 (Cal. Super. Ct. June 9, 1998).

[14] *Robinson v. Shell Oil Co.*, 519 U.S. 337 (1997).

[15] *Robinson v. Shell Oil Co.*, brief for United States and EEOC (as Amici Curiae, pp. 18-21).

The EEOC acted, in part, after noting a vast increase in the number of retaliation claims filed in the previous decade. Retaliation claims may stand alone, but often are filed in conjunction with claims of discrimination, harassment and wrongful discharge. The number of complaints received by the EEOC alleging retaliation has more than doubled in recent years, rocketing from 7,900 claims filed in 1991 to over 18,100 charges in 1998.

The policy guidance, now part of the EEOC's new Compliance Manual issued for use by its investigators when investigating charges of discrimination and retaliation (see Appendix B), gives the retaliation laws an expansive interpretation, greatly increasing protection for employees and, consequently, potential liability for employers.

It is important to note that EEOC policy guidance differs from federal regulations, which are rules issued by federal agencies to implement statutes. Regulations have far greater influence as enforcement tools. Before an agency can issue regulations, a public review and comment period is required. The same review process would be required for the EEOC policy guidance to attain the status of regulations, which could then be established as enforcement guidelines.

Although the Supreme Court has held that EEOC *enforcement guidelines* (as distinguished from EEOC policy guidance) are to be accorded great deference or weight when they support the views of the courts or of Congress on a substantive issue, employers should keep in mind that EEOC policies and guidelines are not binding on the courts. Because the courts' views are largely unsettled on the topic of retaliation, it is difficult to predict how courts will interpret the policy guidance in any particular case.

The Court in *Robinson* did, however, support and accept at least part of the reasoning articulated in the EEOC's amicus brief. The Court specifically agreed with the EEOC's position, later incorporated in its 1998 policy guidance, that both current and former employees are protected by the retaliation provisions of Title VII. It remains to be seen how much more of the EEOC's after-issued guidance on retaliation the Court will accept.

Of course, the EEOC will follow its own policy guidance, which will apply to retaliation actions pursued through the EEOC or state civil rights enforcement agencies. Many courts may also give consideration to the guidance and apply it in whole or in part. It remains to be seen, however, whether courts will closely follow the policy guidance or determine that the EEOC's guidance extends beyond what was intended by Congress or state legislatures in enacting retaliation laws.

The EEOC also has set forth its Charge-Processing Outline in the agency's Compliance Manual, providing an overview of the essential elements of a retaliation claim. This outline allows employers to see exactly how the EEOC will consider the relevant evidence, and to identify the issues with which the commission will be concerned. The outline (see Appendix B) is not applicable to courts' procedures but may be followed in whole or in part by some courts.

Identifying Potential Plaintiffs

Large Class of Potential Plaintiffs

When an employee engages in a protected activity on behalf of another employee or close friend, both the employee and that person may be protected from retaliation. Further, a person complaining of retaliation under Title VII, the ADA, FLSA, ADEA, or EPA need not also allege that he or she was treated differently because of race, religion, sex, national origin, age or disability.[16] In other words, a retaliation plaintiff need not be a member of any of those protected groups. Thus, retaliation provisions of applicable laws serve to create a large class of potential plaintiffs.

Potential Plaintiffs Under ADEA

For example, employers may be surprised to learn that employees under the age of 40 may be protected by the retaliation provisions of the Age Discrimination in Employment Act (ADEA). This fact was brought home to the Phillips Petroleum Company when Craig Anderson, a 32-year-old employee who served as union president at the company's Kansas City facility, was laid off in conjunction with the plant's closing.[17] Anderson, in his position as union president, had filed several charges of age discrimination on behalf of union members over the age of 40, alleging that Phillips was discriminating on the basis of age in its bidding/transfer procedure for jobs at other plants. When the Kansas City facility closed, Anderson was laid off and denied transfer to any of the jobs he had bid on at other plants. Anderson subsequently filed his own ADEA charge against Phillips, alleging that the company had retaliated against him for filing the earlier age bias claims for other workers. A federal jury awarded Anderson $200,000, finding that the company had retaliated against him for filing the age discrimination charges. (This amount was later reduced when the case was remanded to the district court to calculate damages in accordance with a pre-determined formula.)

Phillips argued that the ADEA only applies to those who are at least 40 years of age. The court held, however, that there is no requirement that a plaintiff be at least 40 years old to sue for retaliation under the ADEA. Specifically, the court said that:

> . . . any person, whether or not that person is 40 or older, who participates in or files an age discrimination charge, is protected under the ADEA from retaliation. The purpose of the Act would be abrogated if protection was limited only to those at least 40 years of age.

In reaching its conclusion, the court relied on the EEOC's policy guidance, which clearly states that a person alleging retaliation under the ADEA need not be in the protected age group in order to bring a claim.[18] The only prerequisites for establishing a claim under the ADEA, according to the *Anderson* court, are that the charging party protested employment practices believed to be unlawful under the ADEA or participated in an ADEA investigation, and alleged that the defendant took adverse employment action related to his protest or participation.

Potential Plaintiffs Under ADA

Similarly, employees without disabilities may find protection under the Americans with Disabilities Act (ADA). For example, in one recent case, an employee of American Sterilizer Company who had suffered a work-related back injury was found not to be a "qualified individual with a disability" under the ADA based on his prior assertions of total disability in connection with applications for disability and pension benefits.[19] Although he could not bring a claim of disability discrimination under the ADA, the 3rd U.S. Circuit Court of

---

[16] EEOC Compliance Manual, §8-I(B).

[17] *Anderson v. Phillips Petroleum*, 722 F. Supp. 668 (D. Kan. 1989).

[18] EEOC Compliance Manual, §8-I(B).

[19] *Krouse v. American Sterilizer*, 126 F.3d 494 (3d Cir. 1997).

Appeals found that he could allege that his employer retaliated against him for filing ADA charges with the EEOC. Although the court in this case ultimately ruled that adverse employment actions were not taken in retaliation for the employee's filing a claim with the EEOC, his status as a non-disabled employee would not have prevented his claim. The court said:

> By its own terms, the ADA retaliation provision protects "any individual" who has opposed any act or practice made unlawful by the ADA or who has made a charge under the ADA. This differs from the scope of the ADA disability discrimination provision . . . which may be invoked only by a "qualified individual with a disability." An individual who is adjudged not to be a "qualified individual with a disability" may still pursue a retaliation claim under the ADA.

It is clear that the retaliation provisions of the various laws apply far more broadly than do the discrimination provisions.

Potential Plaintiffs Under Title VII of the Civil Rights Act

Similarly, male employees attempting to assist female co-workers in exercising their Title VII rights also may be protected from retaliation. For example, when a male professor at Indiana State University helped a female professor who was trying to exercise her Title VII rights to keep her job, he was terminated as well.[20] The 7th U.S. Circuit Court of Appeals held that the male professor could properly bring a Title VII claim for retaliation based on Title VII's language prohibiting an "employer to discriminate against any of his employees . . . because he has opposed any practice made an unlawful employment practice by this subchapter, or because he has made a charge, testified, assisted, or participated in any manner in an investigation, proceeding, or hearing under this subchapter." The court said, "We think it clear that this section extends protection to all who 'assist' or 'participate' regardless of their race or sex."

From these applications of law, it is clear that federal discrimination laws offer broad protection from retaliation to many employees, perhaps in situations not often contemplated by employers. These outcomes result from the expansive definition of "protected activity," an essential element of a claim of retaliation.

Potential Plaintiffs in Pre- and Post-Employment Situations

Not only does a large class of potential retaliation plaintiffs exist, but courts have found that plaintiffs can assert retaliation claims before the employment relationship begins and even after the employment relationship has ended (see *Robinson*, discussed at p. 6). They can challenge retaliation by an employer based on protected activity undertaken by the employee in connection with previous employment. For example, this situation might arise when an employee who is disciplined (or an applicant who is not hired) believes that the discipline or failure to hire has occurred because of protected activity the employee (or applicant) engaged in during previous employment.

In reality, when a prospective employer knows that an employee or applicant has sued a previous employer (whether legitimately or not), the subsequent employer may be reluctant to hire that person. No employer would knowingly choose to hire or employ someone who is likely to sue them. Even employees and applicants who have valid claims against previous employers have difficulty getting re-employed because of this fear. An employee or applicant

---

[20] *Eichman v. Indiana State Univ. Bd. of Trustees*, 597 F. 2d 1104 (7th Cir. 1979).

can quite easily frame any disciplinary activity or failure to hire as resulting from retaliation for the earlier protected activity. This potential cause of action may include a claim against both the previous employer for sharing information about the protected activity, or for providing a "negative reference," and the current or prospective employer for allegedly reacting to the negative information.

Potential Plaintiffs Based on Representational Activity

Additionally, employees who are themselves not directly involved in protected activity but who allow a representative to engage in protected activity on their behalf may be able to craft a claim of retaliation.

For example, in 1988, Johnnie Whitfield was fired from his job at Ohio Edison.[21] Soon after, he was offered reinstatement. However, after the offer of reinstatement was made, one of Whitfield's co-workers complained to management about Whitfield's discharge. The co-worker, acting as Whitfield's representative, complained on his behalf, stating that he believed Whitfield had been fired because he was black and that blacks were treated more harshly than whites at Ohio Edison. Soon after the co-worker complained, Ohio Edison withdrew its offer of reinstatement to Whitfield. Whitfield then filed a charge with the EEOC, which filed a complaint on his behalf in federal court.

The 6th U.S. Circuit Court of Appeals said that Whitfield came within the coverage of the statute because he had engaged in protected activity under Title VII by having a representative oppose his discriminatory discharge on his behalf and then suffered retaliation by having an offer of reinstatement withdrawn.

Potential Plaintiffs Based on Close Association

Further, employees can make claims of retaliation based on protected activity undertaken by someone closely related to or associated with them. The EEOC and some courts have taken the position that both members of a married couples may be protected from retaliation even when only one engages in protected activity. In one such case, two press operators who were married to each other were employed by Cadillac Rubber and Plastics.[22] The wife was fired and subsequently sued the company for sexual harassment and sexual discrimination under Title VII.

The husband claimed that the company retaliated against him after his wife filed her claims by disciplining him more harshly than other employees, assigning him to the worst presses (on which he was injured), and referring to him as slow, lazy and incompetent. The court refused to consider his claims that he had "assisted and supported" his wife in pursuing her Title VII claims and that this constituted protected activity. However, the court concluded that the husband had sufficiently stated a claim of retaliation under the law by alleging "protected activity by a close relative, disadvantageous employment action, and a time frame indicating a causal connection between the two."

Broad Employer Liability Exists

Retaliation claims are most often asserted against employers — past, present or prospective. Even where the initial discrimination claims underlying an employee's suit fail, liability still

---

[21] *EEOC v. Ohio Edison Co.*, 7 F.3d 541 (6th Cir. 1993).

[22] EEOC Compliance Manual, §8-II(B)(3)(c); *Murphy v. Cadillac Rubber & Plastics Inc.*, 946 F.Supp. 1108 (W.D.N.Y. 1996).

may be found for supervisors' retaliatory actions taken in response to the original claims of discrimination. For example, the 6th U.S. Circuit Court of Appeals recently found that although a female employee's sexual harassment claims failed, her supervisor's alleged menacing conduct toward her after she complained to their employer was sufficiently severe to be actionable under Title VII's retaliation provisions.[23]

The court was careful to note, however, that because retaliatory harassment does not, in and of itself, constitute a tangible employment action, employers facing a retaliatory harassment claim may assert an affirmative defense based on 1) their exercise of reasonable care to prevent and promptly correct any harassment and 2) the employee's failure to take advantage of available remedies. (See Chapter 3 for a more detailed discussion of affirmative defenses to liability.)

In addition, many discrimination laws — including Title VII, the ADEA and the ADA — provide that employment agencies (such as temporary or placement agencies) and labor unions also can be sued for retaliation.[24] Also, individual liability can be imposed under some laws, such as the ADA and the FLSA.[25] Under these laws, supervisors, managers, officers or others in positions of authority might be sued.

Liability can be imposed even in the absence of unlawful employer practices. For example, the EEOC states that a valid claim for retaliation can exist if the claimant had a reasonable and good faith belief that opposed practices of the employer were unlawful.[26]

This was the case for Laurel Berg, a personnel clerk whose job it was to answer employee questions concerning their rights to disability insurance.[27] During the course of her employment in 1980, Berg told a pregnant employee that she felt the employee was entitled to disability benefits under the law of Wisconsin. Berg also told her employer that she believed the employee was entitled to disability benefits for her pregnancy and that denial of those benefits amounted to sex discrimination. The employer questioned why the company should pay disability benefits "for ten minutes of her fun" and then fired Berg.

In fact, Berg was wrong. At that time, under Wisconsin law, the pregnant employee was not entitled to disability benefits. However, because Berg had relied on information she received about the law at a seminar, the court held that she had a good faith belief that the employer's conduct was unlawful. (The law at that time was unsettled and it was difficult to predict the outcome of a pending U.S. Supreme Court case on the issue. In fact, Title VII subsequently was amended so that withholding disability benefits from pregnant employees now is unlawful.) In deciding Berg's case, the 7th U.S. Circuit Court of Appeals said:

> The plaintiff here was an educated and informed layperson who should not be burdened with the sometimes impossible task of correctly anticipating how the Supreme Court may interpret a particular statute. Even though she was proved wrong . . . [h]er opinion was based upon reasonable belief and her opposition should be protected from retaliatory discharge.

So an employer who, as in this case, has not actually discriminated or committed any wrongdoing may still be successfully sued by an employee who simply did not have all the

---

[23] *Morris v. Oldham County, Ky.*, No. 98-6117 (6th Cir. Jan. 20, 2000).

[24] Title VII, 42 U.S.C.§2000e(b-e); ADEA, 29 U.S.C.§623(b-c); ADA, 42 U.S.C.§§12111(2),(5)(A), and 12112(a).

[25] §503(a) of the ADA.

[26] EEOC Compliance Manual, §8-II(B)(3)(b).

[27] *Berg v. LaCrosse Cooler Co.*, 612 F.2d 1041 (7th Cir. 1980).

relevant facts, or by an employee whose reasonable good faith belief is, in fact, wrong.

Employers also should understand that it is more difficult to successfully defend against a retaliation claim than it is to defend against a discrimination claim. Judges and juries often find it hard to believe that an employer would discriminate against a worker simply because he or she is black, or disabled, for example. But it is much easier to believe, based on our human experience, that an employer may have retaliated against an employee who sued the employer, or who has protested or complained about the employer's actions.

▶ Chapter 2: What Constitutes a Claim of Retaliation?

Retaliation means seeking revenge, evening the score or striking back at a perceived wrong. In the employment law context, examples of retaliation could include termination, suspension, disciplinary action, denial of promotions or benefits or refusal to hire an individual. But, how do we know when these types of relatively common employment actions will lead to a claim of retaliation? Courts are increasingly called upon to determine when an action of this type is justified for work performance or other business reasons, and when it is not, and thus may constitute retaliation.

Essential Elements of a Retaliation Claim

To establish a valid claim of retaliation, a potential plaintiff must prove three elements of the offense. According to the Equal Employment Opportunity Commission (EEOC), a plaintiff can establish a prima facie case of retaliation — in other words, one in which sufficient facts are presented to get the plaintiff past a motion for dismissal — by proving the following three elements:

- that he or she opposed discriminatory employment practices or participated in a covered proceeding (administrative or judicial), referred to as "protected activity";

- that negative or adverse action was taken against the employee; and

- that a relationship or causal connection exists between the protected activity and the adverse action.[1]

Without a showing of each of these required elements, no claim of retaliation can stand. (Each of these elements is discussed separately later in this chapter.) Once a plaintiff has established a prima facie case of retaliation, the burden shifts to the employer to articulate a legitimate nondiscriminatory reason for the adverse action.

There is no requirement in establishing a retaliation claim that the plaintiff be a member of any protected group or class on the basis of race, religion, gender, national origin, age or disability. Generally, we think of protected groups or classes as minorities, women, employees with disabilities and employees over 40 years of age. However, as discussed in Chapter 1, anyone can engage in opposition activity, even if the employment practice complained of does not directly affect them. A white male might refuse to obey an order he believes is discriminatory toward blacks or women. A non-disabled employee might mention to her human resource representative that a disabled employee needs an accommodation. A young salesman might complain to his manager that older employees are not given the best sales territories. A male employee might complain that a pregnant co-worker is not being treated fairly. In all of these cases, the employees involved would be protected against retaliation,

---

[1] EEOC Compliance Manual, §8-II(A).

even though they are not defined as "protected classes" by the relevant statutes and they have not themselves been discriminated against.

Defining Protected Activity

The first element of a claim of retaliation — undertaking protected activity — encompasses both "opposition" activity and "participation" activity.

Opposition activity occurs when an employee opposes a practice of the employer that the employee believes is unlawful under an employment discrimination statute, wage law, or other applicable law.[2] The opposed practice need not actually be unlawful. It is sufficient that the employee have a reasonable and good faith belief that the opposed practice is unlawful.

Participation activity includes making a charge, testifying, assisting or participating in any way in an investigation, hearing, or litigation of a charge of discrimination or other illegal practices whether in court or in administrative proceedings.[3] Participation is protected regardless of whether the underlying charge of discrimination or alleged illegal activity is valid.

Opposition Activity is Protected

How does an employee engage in opposition activity? Opposition encompasses any explicit or implicit communication to an employer or other entity of a belief that discriminatory or unlawful activity has occurred. This would include, for example, an informal comment or statement that the employee believes that discrimination has occurred in the workplace, or that unsafe conditions exist in the workplace. In addition to covering complaints of discrimination in employment practices or in the workplace, the Americans with Disabilities Act also prohibits discrimination in the provision of government services, public accommodations and telecommunications.[4] Consequently, under the ADA, an employee could complain about the accessibility of telephones or restrooms in a hospital, or ATMs in a bank, and be protected from retaliation.

According to the EEOC, opposition activities include the following:

- threatening to file a charge or complaint of discrimination, whether with a union, an administrative agency or in court;

- refusing to obey an order of the employer because of a reasonable belief that it is discriminatory;

- requesting reasonable accommodation or religious accommodation; and

- merely complaining to anyone explicitly or implicitly about a perception of unlawful employment discrimination. The discrimination need not be specifically labeled as such; it need only be communicated so that it could reasonably be interpreted as opposition to discrimination. This includes nonverbal activities such as lock-ins, lock-outs, work slow-downs, sick-outs or picketing.[5]

---

[2] EEOC Compliance Manual, §8-II(B)(1).
[3] EEOC Compliance Manual, §8-II(C)(1).
[4] Americans with Disabilities Act (ADA), 42 U.S.C. §12132.
[5] EEOC Compliance Manual, §8-II(B)(2).

Additionally, if an employee complains on behalf of another, the EEOC views this as constituting protected opposition activity on behalf of both the person making the complaint and the person on whose behalf the complaint is made.[6]

Clearly, opposition activities are given a broad interpretation by the EEOC. For example, allowing claims by employees who have complained on behalf of other employees gives almost anyone a cause of action with very little warning to the employer. The EEOC policy guidance also expressly states that even "broad or ambiguous complaints of unfair treatment" will constitute opposition activity.[7] The policy guidance does not even require that complaints of discrimination be made to management or to enforcement officials; under the guidance, complaints or protests may be made to "anyone," including co-workers, attorneys, newspaper reporters or elected officials. [8]

Courts Interpret Opposition Activity

We know that the EEOC defines opposition activity quite broadly, but how have the courts defined it? Examples of opposition activity that has been protected by various courts include:

- informal complaints;

- failure to follow an unlawful order;

- requesting accommodation for a disability;

- lodging an internal complaint; and

- vague complaints.

Informal Complaints

Generally, the courts (and of course, the EEOC) have stated that federal laws prohibiting job discrimination should be given broad, remedial effect.[9] To this end, the courts have said that these laws must protect even those employees who have not actually filed a claim with an administrative agency or the courts. For example, in one recent case, the 1st U.S. Circuit Court of Appeals found that merely writing a note to a supervisor stating that the employee was "considering complaint options" and had contacted the U.S. Department of Labor (DOL) was enough to trigger protection under the Fair Labor Standards Act's (FLSA's) retaliation provisions.[10] Also protected are employees who have completely bypassed the internal complaint or grievance system.[11]

If the law were not interpreted this way, employees might be hesitant to discuss potential problems or claims with employers (without first filing a claim) for fear of retaliation. This would prevent possible early settlements or resolutions, which benefit both parties. If those making informal complaints were not protected in this manner, employers would actually have an incentive to safely fire employees as soon as an employee complained or indicated

---

[6] *Id.*

[7] *Id.*

[8] *Id.*

[9] EEOC Compliance Manual, §8-II(D)(3).

[10] *Valerio v. Putnam Associates Inc.,* 173 F.3d 35 (1st Cir. 1999).

[11] EEOC Compliance Manual, §8-II(B)(2).

any concern, and before the employee had any chance to file a charge (after which time the employee would be protected).

The EEOC also says, and many courts agree, that even internal, nonspecific complaints constitute protected opposition activity.[12] In one case, for example, a temporary custodian complained to her school district employer that she believed the district was "breaking some sort of law" by paying her lower wages than were previously paid to male temporary custodians.[13] She was not called back for any other temporary assignments at the school, nor was she considered for permanent custodial positions. Because these adverse employment actions followed her complaints about her pay, the 6th U.S. Circuit Court of Appeals found a causal connection and held that she had effectively set forth a claim of retaliation. Even though she had not actually filed a formal claim or complaint, did not cite a specific law, and may or may not have had a legitimate claim of wage discrimination, she did have a legitimate claim of retaliation, according to the court.

In another, more recent case, six ticket salespeople for the Seattle SuperSonics basketball team complained to their supervisors of not receiving proper overtime compensation.[14] Their employer threatened to fire them for complaining and then did so. The 9th U.S. Circuit Court of Appeals subsequently ruled that the employees were protected, even though they had only made informal complaints to their supervisors, and awarded the ticket agents $5.3 million. The U.S. Supreme Court declined review of the case, so the award stood.

Failure to Follow an Unlawful Order

Refusing to obey an order from the employer also constitutes protected opposition if the individual reasonably believes that the order requires him or her to carry out unlawful employment discrimination. For example, one such case arose when six employees of a national child care chain were injured in a car accident while on company business.[15] They all filed workers' compensation claims, and some consulted attorneys. Their employer did not want their injuries reflected in the company's records and considered their actions disloyal. The employer ordered a supervisor to fire the six employees, but she refused. Soon afterward, the supervisor received her first negative performance review and was placed on job probation. She was then terminated. In the ensuing court action, a Washington state appeals court found that the order to terminate the six employees was illegal. Thus, the court held that the supervisor's termination was retaliatory.

In a similar case, a black prison guard protested and refused to follow a prison policy allowing only white inmates to shower after work shifts.[16] He was then fired and later sued his employer, claiming that his discharge resulted from his protests against the policy and his refusal to enforce the policy. The 9th U.S. Circuit Court of Appeals found that he was protected as engaging in opposition activity.

Requesting Accommodation for a Disability

A request for reasonable accommodation of a disability constitutes protected activity under Section 503 of the Americans with Disabilities Act. Although a person making such a

---

[12] *Id.*

[13] *EEOC v. Romeo Community School Dist.*, 976 F.2d 985 (6th Cir. 1992).

[14] *Lambert v. Ackerly*, 5 Wage & Hour Cas. 2d 677 (9th Cir. 1999), *cert. denied*, No. 99-681 (U.S., Jan. 18, 2000).

[15] *Lins v. Children's Discovery Center*, 976 P.2d 168 (Wash. Ct. App., May 7, 1999).

[16] *Moyo v. Gomez*, 40 F.3d 982 (9th Cir. 1994), *cert. denied*, 513 U.S. 1081 (1995).

request might not literally "oppose" discrimination or "participate" in the administrative or judicial complaint process, he or she is protected against retaliation for making the request. For example, a customer service administrator whose primary function involved typing and who requested a split keyboard or voice-activated computer to accommodate a nerve disability was protected, a federal district court found.[17]

Interestingly, an employee's request for accommodation of a disability constitutes protected activity even if the employee wouldn't actually qualify for accommodation, or if the requested accommodation would pose an undue hardship for the employer.

Persons requesting religious accommodation under Title VII also are protected against retaliation for making such requests.

Lodging An Internal Complaint

Complaining of alleged employment discrimination to a manager, co-worker or company equal employment opportunity official constitutes opposition activity. For example, a black postal worker who complained and wrote a letter to his supervisor stating that preferred routes were being assigned to letter carriers on a racially discriminatory basis was found to be protected.[18]

Other likely examples of protected opposition activity would include threatening to file a discrimination complaint or wage and hour claim, complaining about unequal pay between the genders, and making an internal complaint of sexual harassment.

Vague Complaints

Even though an employee's complaints are not required to specifically cite applicable laws that the employee believes are being violated, complaints must be stated so that they can "reasonably" be interpreted as opposition to employment discrimination or other unlawful activity.[19] Courts vary in their interpretation of this "reasonableness" requirement. In explaining the concept of reasonable interpretation, the EEOC manual presents a hypothetical involving a female employee who complains to her foreman about workplace graffiti that is derogatory toward women. Although she does not specify that she believes the graffiti creates a hostile work environment based on sex, her complaint reasonably should be interpreted by the foreman as opposition to sex discrimination due to the sex-based content of the graffiti.[20]

Another case, however, focused on a letter written by a transportation clerk complaining of generally "unfair" treatment and expressing dissatisfaction that another employee received a position for which the clerk had applied.[21] The second employee happened to be younger than the clerk, but the letter did not specifically refer to age discrimination. The 3rd U.S. Circuit Court of Appeals found that the letter was simply "too vague" to constitute the required "protected activity" needed to make a claim for retaliation.

Limits on Opposition Activity: It Must Be 'Reasonable'

The EEOC and the courts have limited protection of opposition activity to that which is "reasonable." Opposition is reasonable, and thus protected, if it is based on a good faith

---

[17] *Garza v. Abbott Laboratories*, 940 F. Supp. 1227 (N.D. Ill. 1996).

[18] *Sumner v. U.S. Postal Service*, 899 F.2d 203 (2d Cir. 1990).

[19] EEOC Compliance Manual, §8-II(B)(2).

[20] *Id.*

[21] *Barber v. CSX Distrib. Services*, 68 F.3d 694 (3d Cir. 1995).

belief that the opposed practices are illegal. Further, the opposition activity itself must be legal in order to be protected. Thus, any opposition activity that is illegal, such as vandalism or violence, is not protected.

In determining the reasonableness of opposition activity and whether it is based on good faith belief, decisions will be made on a case-by-case basis. To be reasonable, employees' protests may not unduly interfere with job performance.[22] If an employee's protests against allegedly discriminatory employment render him or her ineffective in the job, the retaliation provisions do not immunize the worker from appropriate discipline or discharge. The courts will engage in a balancing test. On the one hand, courts must consider the purpose of retaliation provisions combined with the need to protect the rights of individual employees asserting their rights under these provisions. On the other hand, courts must consider an employer's legitimate demands for loyalty, cooperation and a generally productive work environment as well as control of its personnel.[23]

Also, appropriate discipline or discharge procedures may still be undertaken by the employer. The courts will continue to balance the rights of individuals to oppose discrimination or unlawful activity with employers' rights to conduct productive businesses.

What Constitutes Unreasonable Opposition?

Although the opposition clause in each of the EEO statutes is broad, it does not protect every protest against job discrimination. Courts have found that a number of unreasonable or unlawful activities fall outside the scope of protected activity. In one such case, a 42-year-old employee was denied a promotion to lead engineer at a McDonnell Douglas Helicopter Company plant in Arizona.[24] The employee was convinced that he was denied the promotion because of his age. The night after he was denied the promotion, he searched his supervisor's office, photocopied several confidential documents that he believed supported his belief that the company discriminated on the basis of age, and later showed the documents to a co-worker.

The 9th U.S. Circuit Court of Appeals found that the employee's activity was not reasonable and thus did not constitute protected activity, stating that:

> [W]e are loathe to provide employees an incentive to rifle through confidential files looking for evidence that might come in handy in later litigation. The opposition clause protects reasonable attempts to contest an employer's discrimination practices; it is not an insurance policy, a license to flout company rules or an invitation to dishonest behavior.

Similarly, conduct that is extremely disruptive or inappropriate has been found to be outside the scope of protected activity. In one such case, an employee habitually bypassed the chain of command in complaining about discrimination.[25] Further, her complaints were frequent and frivolous and she often expressed her complaints in an insubordinate and antagonistic manner, such as calling her supervisor a "fool." Even though the employee was complaining about discrimination, which would ordinarily be a clear example of opposition

---

[22] EEOC Compliance Manual, §8-II(B)(3)(a).

[23] *Rollins v. Florida Dep't of Law Enforcement*, 868 F.2d 397 (11th Cir. 1989); *O'Day v. McDonnell Douglas Helicopter Co.*, 79 F.3d 756 (9th Cir. 1996).

[24] *O'Day v. McDonnell Douglas Helicopter Co.*, 79 F.3d 756 (9th Cir. 1996).

[25] *Rollins v. Florida Dep't of Law Enforcement*, 868 F.2d 397 (11th Cir. 1989).

activity, the 11th U.S. Circuit Court of Appeals found that the hostile and disruptive manner in which she complained of discrimination "transgressed the bonds of protection." It is difficult to predict when opposition activity will be considered reasonable, and when it will not. Answers will vary by jurisdiction.

Customer Letters

As discussed above, the reasonableness of opposition activity will always be determined on a case-by-case basis, depending on the specific facts involved. However, in determining what type of opposition activity is "reasonable", and thus protected, at least one very disturbing category of opposition activity exists. The EEOC Compliance Manual states that public criticism of alleged discrimination may be a reasonable form of opposition. For example, some courts have protected an employee's right to inform an employer's customers about the employer's alleged discrimination as well as the right to engage in peaceful picketing to oppose allegedly discriminatory employment practices.[26]

One very disturbing decision in this regard came from the 9th U.S. Circuit Court of Appeals in 1983.[27] Over the course of several years, black employees in a Los Angeles warehouse filed discrimination complaints with the EEOC, picketed the company, and wrote complaint letters to elected officials as well as to the chairman of their employer, Crown Zellerbach Corporation. Finally, in 1979, the employees wrote a letter protesting racism and discrimination at Crown, and mailed it to one of the company's most significant customers. The company was rightfully concerned about how the customer might respond and fired the employees who signed the letter. Although the 9th Circuit acknowledged that the employees' conduct was disloyal, the court went on to say that "[a]lmost every form of 'opposition to an unlawful employment practice' is in some sense 'disloyal' to the employer, since it entails a disagreement with the employer's views and a challenge to the employer's policies. Otherwise, the conduct would not be 'opposition.' If discharge or other disciplinary sanctions may be imposed based simply on 'disloyal' conduct, it is difficult to see what opposition would remain protected . . .." In specifically finding the employee's actions to be reasonable opposition and protected activity, the court found no effect "upon the workplace environment."

This is a particularly difficult issue for employers. The EEOC and the courts in the cases noted above have said that employees can write critical, damaging letters to their employers' customers (which might not have any basis in fact, because the employee need only act in good faith), and that this may constitute reasonable opposition activity. However, negative customer communications could be completely devastating to an employer's business. An employer cannot prohibit employees from engaging in this type of communication nor can it punish employees for doing so, but it must somehow counteract any negative public relations impact caused by the communication. This is an extremely unfavorable result for employers and unfortunately not one that can be easily avoided.

Is Employer Knowledge of Opposition Activity Required?

The EEOC does not specifically require knowledge by the employer of opposition activity as an element of a retaliation claim. It may reasonably be assumed, however, that liability for retaliatory conduct may not be imposed on an employer unless it knew of an employee's

---

[26] EEOC Compliance Manual, §8-II(B)(3)(a); *Sumner v. United States Postal Service*, 899 F.2d 203 (2d Cir. 1990).

[27] *EEOC v. Crown Zellerbach Corp.*, 720 F.2d 1008 (9th Cir. 1983).

participation in a protected activity. Otherwise, an employer could be held liable for retaliating against an employee, even if it was unaware that the employee had taken any action the employer might wish to retaliate against.

Some courts have specifically added employer knowledge as a fourth element, requiring that a defendant employer be aware of the protected activity asserted. In other words, several federal appellate courts have required a plaintiff claiming retaliation to show:

1. that the plaintiff engaged in protected activity;

2. that the plaintiff's involvement in protected activity was known to the employer;

3. that, thereafter, the employer took an employment action adverse to the employee; and

4. that there was a relationship or causal connection between the protected activity and the adverse employment action.[28]

The widespread adoption of this additional requirement by courts would be very helpful to employer defendants. Arguments should be presented on this issue in any court proceeding in which the employer's knowledge regarding the existence of protected activity is at issue. This additional element may be crucial to successfully defending a case.

The EEOC seems to indicate, by omitting employer knowledge as a required element for a claim of retaliation, that it would impose liability even if a defendant employer had no knowledge that an employee or applicant had engaged in protected activity. This approach obviously poses a far greater risk to employers than if knowledge of the protected activity is required. In practice, allowing plaintiffs to make retaliation claims against employers who are unaware that something has occurred to retaliate against is impractical and thus far, most courts have refused to do so.

Participation Activity Is Protected

As stated earlier, participation is protected regardless of whether the underlying charge of discrimination or alleged illegal activity is valid. Thus, the EEOC's position on participation activity differs significantly from its position on opposition activity in one important respect: the employee does not need to have any reasonable or good faith belief in the validity of a charge of discrimination or illegal activity to be protected for participation activities. Even if a charge of discrimination or illegal activity is completely baseless or unreasonable, the plaintiff is still protected from retaliation. The employee is protected even if he or she is mistaken,[29] and even if the employee's charge is malicious and defamatory.[30] Protection for participation applies to all who participate in any manner in the statutory complaint process.[31] This could actually encourage employees who are being disciplined or whose performance is unsatisfactory to file a baseless claim against the employer, thereby setting up a potential retaliation claim if they are further disciplined or discharged.

Additionally, the EEOC has said that a potential retaliation plaintiff need not even be the person who engaged in participation activity.[32] As is true with opposition activity, if a

---

[28] *Wrenn v. Gould*, 808 F.2d 493,500 (6th Cir. 1987); *Burrus v. United Telephone Co.*, 683 F.2d 339 (10th Cir. 1981), *cert. denied*, 459 U.S. 1071 (1982); *Smalley v. City of Eatonville*, 640 F.2d 76 (5th Cir. 1981); *Womack v. Munson*, 619 F.2d 1292 (8th Cir. 1980), *cert. denied*, 450 U.S. 979 (1981); *Grant v. Bethlehem Steel Corp.*, 622 F.2d 43 (2d Cir. 1980).

[29] *Womack v. Munson*, 619 F.2d 1292 (8th Cir. 1980), *cert. denied*, 450 U.S. 9791 (1981).

[30] *Pettway v. American Cast Iron Pipe Co.*, 411 F.2d 998 (5th Cir. 1969).

[31] EEOC Compliance Manual, §8-II(C)(2); *Wyatt v. City of Boston*, 35 F.3d 13 (1st Cir. 1994).

[32] EEOC Compliance Manual, §8-II(C)(3).

potential plaintiff is closely related to or associated with someone who has engaged in participation activity, both persons would be protected from retaliation. Thus, relatives, those involved in committed relationships and possibly even close friends would be protected against retaliation by a common employer, even if only one party had engaged in participation activity.[33]

Protection against retaliation for participation can lead to some surprising results. For instance, Dillard Paper Company was sued by its receptionist, who alleged that five men had sexually harassed her.[34] The five men were deposed in the course of the suit, and one salesman, Harry Merritt, admitted to several incidents of harassing the receptionist as well as other female employees. The company settled the case with the receptionist, then focused on disciplining the five harassers. Merritt was fired after being told by the company president that his "deposition was the most damning to Dillard's case."

Merritt then sued the company himself, claiming that he had been fired in retaliation for his deposition testimony in the receptionist's case. The 11th U.S. Circuit Court of Appeals found that his deposition testimony was protected participation activity, even though he had not voluntarily assisted the receptionist in pursuit of her civil rights. Although he had involuntarily "participated" in her Title VII claim of harassment by reluctantly and defensively giving deposition testimony, this still constituted protected participation activity, which prevented retaliation by the employer, according to the court.

The court found that Merritt presented sufficient evidence to argue that he was fired due to his participation in his deposition rather than his sexually harassing behavior. The court, considering the company president's statement to Merritt about his deposition to be direct evidence of retaliation, reluctantly found that Merritt must be allowed to proceed to trial with his retaliation claim.

This case illustrates the difficulty employers face in disciplining errant employees without running afoul of retaliation provisions. Here the company arguably had relied on Merritt's sworn testimony admitting that he sexually harassed female employees and discharged him. Had Merritt not been discharged, the company could have faced additional liability stemming from any further harassment of female employees by Merritt. And yet, because of the president's choice of words in discharging him, the company wound up defending itself against an admitted harasser. Presumably, had the company president chosen his words more carefully, it would have been harder for Merritt to prove his case against the company.

If the company president had said that Merritt was being fired for his admitted sexual harassment, the court indicated the discharge would have been upheld. The court also said that even if Merritt won his retaliation claim at trial, it would be a pyrrhic victory for him: if the employer could convince the factfinder that it would have fired him in the absence of a retaliatory motive, Merritt would not receive damages or reinstatement (see employer defenses in Chapter 3). Here, the company is likely to be able to show that even if it had not retaliated against Merritt, he still would properly have been fired for sexual harassment.

This reasoning is disturbing as it could result in prolonged, expensive and unnecessary litigation for employers. The court seemed to recognize the flawed result, stating that it could not refuse to give effect to the applicable law "merely because we think Congress has acted

---

[33] *Thurman v. Robertshaw Controls Co.*, 869 F.Supp. 934 (N.D. Ga. 1994). (Plaintiff's wife filed a charge of sex discrimination with the EEOC, so plaintiff had engaged in protected activity as well.)

[34] *Merritt v. Dillard Paper Co.*, 120 F.3d 1181 (11th Cir. 1997).

unwisely." Even though an employer might ultimately prevail in such a case, the better approach is to carefully discipline and discharge employees (when necessary) to avoid wasteful and unproductive litigation.

One message is clear from this case. Disciplining or discharging employees who have engaged in protected activity must be done very carefully and precisely and should be well-documented. (Suggestions for handling similar situations are included in Chapter 4.)

Types of Adverse Action

In addition to a plaintiff's participation in protected activity, at least two additional elements are required to sustain a claim for retaliation. Adverse action, the second requirement or element of a claim of retaliation, is action that is damaging, harmful, detrimental or injurious to the potential plaintiff. In other words, any employment decision that would be viewed as negatively affecting an employee or applicant could be considered an adverse action. Firing or disciplining an employee, denying promotions or benefits, or failing to hire a job applicant are all examples of negative or adverse action. Once an employee has engaged in protected activity, virtually any negative action—including shift changes, relocation of offices, decreases in administrative support or benefits—could form the basis for a claim of retaliation.

Courts have also found adverse action where an employer has refused to allow a plaintiff, who has sued the employer in court or in an administrative action, to use the employer's grievance procedure. In one case, a collective bargaining agreement provided that an internal grievance procedure could be bypassed if the employee sued the employer.[35] In another case, a union refused to proceed with an employee's grievance after he filed a race discrimination claim with his state civil rights enforcement agency.[36] In both cases, the courts held that losing the right to use an in-house grievance proceeding was an adverse action penalizing the employee who engaged in protected participation activity.

It is also possible that adverse action may support a claim of retaliation even when it is unrelated to the terms and conditions of employment. Some courts have said that even when retaliatory acts are unrelated to employment, they may be actionable simply because they are committed by an employer.

For instance, a clerk of Mexican descent, Alfredo Aviles, claimed that his supervisors discriminated against him and harassed him on the basis of his national origin.[37] He filed charges with the EEOC. Minutes after he told his supervisors of the charges, he received a five-day suspension. His supervisor also made a false report to the police, stating that the clerk was armed and lying in wait for the supervisor outside the plant. The police, believing the false report, arrested Aviles, allegedly injuring him so severely in the process that he was unable to work for six weeks.

A lower court held that the clerk's subsequent retaliation claim was barred because the police action had no adverse effect on the clerk's employment. On appeal, however, the 7th U.S. Circuit Court of Appeals found that the fact that the supervisor made the false report to the police within minutes of learning of the EEOC charges was sufficient evidence of

---

[35] *EEOC v. Board of Governors of State Colleges and Universities*, 957 F.2d 424 (7th Cir. 1992), *cert. denied*, 506 U.S. 906 (1992).

[36] *Johnson v. Palma*, 931 F.2d 203 (2d Cir. 1991).

[37] *Aviles v. Cornell Forge Co.*, 183 F.3d 598 (7th Cir. 1999).

retaliation. "A false report to the police that Aviles was armed and lying in wait outside the plant could certainly be construed as a retaliatory action meant to discourage Aviles from pursuing his claim," the appellate court held. The employee was allowed to proceed to trial on his retaliation claim.

More problematic for employers, however, is what other, less obvious conduct will be considered by the courts to rise to a level serious enough to be considered retaliation. This less obvious conduct may arise from the way an employee is treated in the workplace. Examples of this type of retaliation could include threats, harassment, isolation or other adverse treatment in the workplace. It could also include more subtle forms of retaliation such as ignoring an employee, talking negatively about an employee, spreading rumors or simply being unkind. Although the EEOC has said that "petty slights and trivial annoyances" would not constitute actionable retaliation[38], it is not clear where courts will draw the line.

It is easy to see how difficult it is for employers to guard against these more subtle forms of retaliation. For example, if a female employee accuses a male of sexual harassment, it is understandable that other male employees might be reluctant to interact with her. However, this more limited interaction, which may in turn result in more limited employment opportunities for her, could constitute adverse action, especially if the employer's managers or supervisors participate in or encourage this behavior.

Some courts have upheld these types of claims, allowing "hostile environment" retaliation claims (similar to sexual harassment hostile environment claims) to go forward. For example, Lorey Ann Davis, a secretary in a Little Rock, Ark., trucking office, filed a sexual harassment complaint with the EEOC. Afterward, she said the company retaliated against her by nitpicking her work, imposing additional requirements for taking medical leave, and falsely accusing her of rude behavior toward customers and taking unexcused absences from work. The court held the trucking company liable for this hostile environment retaliation.[39] Threats are also a common form of retaliation prohibited by the EEOC and some courts, even when they do not materially affect the terms and conditions of employment.[40]

The involvement of managers or supervisors in retaliatory harassment can greatly increase an employer's potential liability. The 10th U.S. Circuit Court of Appeals held in 1998 that an employer could be liable for retaliatory harassment by co-workers when its supervisors or managers either 1) orchestrate the harassment or 2) know about it and acquiesce in such a manner as to condone and encourage it.[41] In this case, a secretary filed grievances and a complaint of sexual harassment against her employer, Utah Valley State College. Afterward, co-workers treated her badly, made false accusations against her, tried to make it appear that she was negligent in performing her duties, and left her out of communications. Despite this behavior on the part of the secretary's co-workers, however, there was no evidence that supervisors or managers orchestrated or even knew of these retaliatory actions. Consequently, the appellate court found that the employer was not liable for retaliation.

Even when it can be shown that a supervisor or manager is involved in the retaliatory harassment, however, the harassment must be severe or pervasive to be actionable — a similar

---

[38] EEOC Compliance Manual, §8-II(D)(3).

[39] *Davis v. Tri-State Mack Distributors Inc.*, 981 F.2d 340 (8th Cir. 1992).

[40] EEOC Compliance Manual, §8-II(D)(3); *McKnight v. General Motors Corp.*, 908 F.2d 104 (7th Cir. 1990), *cert. denied*, 499 U.S. 919 (1999); *Garcia v. Lawn*, 805 F.2d 1400 (9th Cir. 1986); *Atkinson v. Oliver T. Carr Co.*, 40 FEP Cases (BNA) (D. D.C. 1986).

[41] *Gunnell v. Utah Valley State College*, 152 F.3d 1253 (10th Cir. 1998).

standard to that applied in sexual harassment cases. For example, the 6th U.S. Circuit Court of Appeals applied this standard in a case involving an electric meter service installer, Shelly Richmond-Hopes, who alleged that she was retaliated against after filing a sexual harassment claim.[42] The retaliation included being assigned to more dangerous work than she was qualified to perform, being deprived of overtime, being ignored and being called a "bitch." The court found, however, that each time Richmond-Hopes had complained to her employer, the retaliatiory conduct was corrected. She experienced no demotion, no change in title, nor any change in pay or benefits after filing her harassment claim. The appellate court found that because Richmond-Hopes suffered no tangible, adverse employment action, "the city can assert an affirmative defense by showing that it exercised reasonable care to prevent and correct promptly any retaliatory behavior and that the plaintiff unreasonably failed to take advantage of preventive and corrective opportunities provided by the employer." Therefore, Richmond-Hopes' claim of retaliatory harassment failed, according to the court.

Constructive Discharge

Employers are often surprised when employees who have quit or resigned sue them for retaliation. Employers may believe that employees who voluntarily choose to quit have no basis for a claim of discrimination or retaliation because the employer took no adverse action. However, this is not always true. Employees who choose to quit may still have viable claims based on "constructive discharge," a legal concept that treats the employer as if the employee had been fired. A constructive discharge arises when an employer makes the work environment so unpleasant for an employee that the employee is, in effect, fired against his or her will even though the employee "voluntarily" resigns.

In fact, the very same factual allegations may be used to support both a claim for retaliation and a claim for constructive discharge. For example, a plaintiff might allege that after complaining about sexual harassment or some other illegal activity, he or she was treated poorly in retaliation for the complaint, and thereby forced to resign. The following case illustrates how workplace conduct can be construed as retaliation and can also lead to a claim of constructive discharge when the employee quits.

After bringing allegations of sexual harassment to the attention of management, a female bank employee claimed that her co-workers ostracized her.[43] She claimed that she overheard inappropriate comments linking her name and the alleged harasser's. One male co-worker stopped eating lunch with her because he said it might be "damaging" to be seen with her. Another male supervisor allegedly said she couldn't transfer to his department because he liked to joke with the women in his department. The male president of the company allegedly began to avoid her and asked her to use the back stairs when meetings were necessary. She also complained of discomfort when customers called with inquiries regarding the departed alleged harasser. The female human resources officer responded by telling her to "tough it out."

The employee used these allegations as the basis of a constructive discharge claim and the court construed them as supporting an additional retaliation claim. However, the U.S. District Court for Southern Ohio ultimately ruled in favor of the employer on both claims,

---

[42] *Richmond-Hopes v. City of Cleveland*, 168 F.3d 490 (6th Cir. 1998); citing with approval, *Burlington Industries v. Ellerth*, 524 U.S. 742 (1998).

[43] *Hall v. Hebrank*, C-3-95-430 (S.D. Ohio, Jan. 19, 1999).

finding that the employer had not "orchestrated a campaign to retaliate" against her, nor had it condoned or encouraged the retaliatory conduct, nor created an atmosphere unpleasant enough to compel the plaintiff to resign.

In a similar case, an Ohio state appeals court found no constructive discharge when an assistant manager at a Friendly's restaurant was treated hostilely upon her return from workers' compensation leave.[44] The assistant manager, Tracy Risch, had informed her manager that she needed additional time off to recover from her work-related injury. The manager had responded that she was "a goddamn baby," implied that she was a malingerer, and complained that she was costing the restaurant money with her workers' compensation claim. He also allegedly said that the two could no longer work in the same restaurant and that he would not be the one to leave. Risch then resigned and filed a complaint alleging wrongful discharge. The court held that the manager's comments were not so egregious or pervasive as to render Risch's work environment intolerable. Specifically, the court stated that "[h]aving a difficult boss is not constructive discharge. If it were, the unemployment lines, and the court dockets, would be long indeed."

In another case, however, where the same factual allegations were used to support both a claim of retaliation and a claim of constructive discharge, the plaintiff was successful.[45] In the case, Delores Beckwith had been a sales manager with Dillard Department Stores for about 25 years when she strained her back at work and required time off to recover. Before she was released by her doctor to return to work, the store manager asked her to return and she declined. Dillard's then filled her job with another manager. When Beckwith did return to work, she was given a choice of resigning or accepting a permanent entry-level sales position with a 40 percent cut in pay and benefits, despite the availability of two other sales manager positions for which she was qualified. She complained to management about the lower-level position and the humiliation of the demotion, but to no avail; she was told that her demotion was directly related to her workers' comp claim. She resigned one week before her 25th anniversary as an employee and pursued retaliation and constructive discharge claims. A jury found the employer liable for intentional infliction of emotional distress and awarded Beckwith damages of nearly $2.5 million, which the Nevada Supreme Court upheld.

How Bad Does the Adverse Action Have to Be?

The question of just how bad adverse treatment in the workplace has to be to rise to a level serious enough to constitute retaliation is still unresolved. Can a plaintiff prevail if any adverse or negative treatment occurs or only if the adverse treatment is significant, material or fairly substantial? Or must the adverse treatment constitute an "ultimate" employment action such as discharge or demotion? This is a troubling and significant issue with which courts continue to grapple.

The EEOC has said that a plaintiff need only show adverse treatment that "is reasonably likely to deter the charging party or others from engaging in protected activity."[46] Although the EEOC has said that "petty slights" and "trivial annoyances" would not be enough for an actionable claim,[47] this is a fairly minimal standard of proof, requiring only a minor amount

---

[44] *Risch v. Friendly's Ice Cream Corp.*, No. C-990037 (Ohio Ct. App., Hamilton Cty., Oct. 1, 1999).

[45] *Dillard Dep't Stores Inc. v. Beckwith*, 989 P.2d 882 (Nev., Dec. 13, 1999).

[46] EEOC Compliance Manual, §8-II(D)(3).

[47] *Id.*

of harm or less serious consequences. Thus, the EEOC's position is that almost regardless of the amount or seriousness of harm, nearly any retaliation deters potential plaintiffs from filing charges and should therefore be actionable.

Courts generally have imposed more stringent standards of proof requiring evidence of more serious harm. Some courts have even held that plaintiffs must show retaliation that rises to the level of an ultimate employment action, such as discharge or demotion. These courts have held that adverse employment actions such as harassment, reprimands, poor evaluations or reassignments did not rise to the level of an "ultimate employment action" sufficient to constitute retaliation.[48]

In one case, for example, a female mechanic for Eastman Kodak filed a charge of sexual harassment with the EEOC.[49] After she filed the charge, her work was reviewed more negatively, and she was reprimanded, placed on "final warning," verbally threatened with termination and visited by supervisors at her home. Also, her co-workers were hostile to her, refusing to say "hello," and her locker was broken into and some of her tools stolen. Even this laundry list of complaints, the 5th U.S. Circuit Court of Appeals held, was not enough to constitute actionable conduct. Retaliation provisions set forth in Title VII were "designed to address ultimate employment decisions, not to address every decision made by employers that arguably might have some tangential effect upon those ultimate decisions," the court said.

Other courts have adopted a less stringent standard with regard to the severity of adverse action required to sustain a retaliation claim, but have still required employees to at least show that an adverse action has materially or tangibly affected the terms, conditions or privileges of their employment. For example, one court found no employer liability for retaliation, although the employer had encouraged other workers to shun the employee, spy on her and report to management about her activities.[50] The court held that these activities, even though condoned and in fact encouraged by the employer, did not adversely affect the terms, conditions or benefits of the worker's employment and so could not support a claim of retaliation.

In yet another case, the 6th U.S. Circuit Court of Appeals refused to allow a retaliation claim to stand, finding that the alleged adverse action was not serious enough to rise to a material level of harm.[51] The case involved a black, female employee who wore various hairstyles to work that her employer described as "too different," "eye-catching," and "too drastic." She was required to get pre-approval for her hairstyles, but white employees were not. When she was told that her failure to wear a "correct" hairstyle would affect her reviews, she filed discrimination charges, which constituted protected participation activity.

The court said she might have a claim for discrimination, but not one for retaliation. Although her performance evaluations were slightly lower after filing the charge, the court ruled that this was not a material adverse change in the terms and conditions of her employment sufficient to support a claim of retaliation.

The requirement that adverse action be sufficiently material or substantial is common in other types of discrimination cases.[52] It is also a critical element in sexual harassment cases.

---

[48] *Mattern v. Eastman Kodak Co.*, 104 F.3d 702 (5th Cir. 1997), *cert. denied*, 522 U.S. 932 (1997); *Ledergerber v. Stangler*, 122 F.3d 1142 (8th Cir. 1997).

[49] *Mattern v. Eastman Kodak Co.*, 104 F.3d 702 (5th Cir. 1997), *cert. denied*, 522 U.S. 932 (1997).

[50] *Munday v. Waste Management*, 126 F.3d 239 (4th Cir. 1997), *cert. denied*, 522 U.S. 1116 (1998).

[51] *Hollins v. Atlantic Co.*, 188 F.3d 652 (6th Cir. 1999).

[52] *Rogers v. EEOC*, 454 F.2d 234 (5th Cir. 1971), *cert. denied*, 406 U.S. 957 (1972).

For example, a plaintiff who can successfully demonstrate that sexual harassment has occurred still must show some material, tangible effect on employment or the employer will be allowed to raise an affirmative defense (see Chapter 3).[53]

The EEOC and some courts disagree with the various courts that have decided this issue as described above. The EEOC and these courts have specifically said that liability can be established even when there has been no material effect on a plaintiff's job.[54] The EEOC makes a distinction between retaliation claims and other types of discrimination claims on the basis of the broad language of the various statutory retaliation provisions. These retaliation provisions prohibit "any action" that is reasonably likely to prevent someone from complaining about alleged discrimination.[55] The EEOC interprets "any action" as an unqualified prohibition of all adverse treatment that is reasonably likely to deter protected activity.

In contrast, discrimination provisions of those same statutes refer specifically to prohibitions of actions affecting the "terms, conditions, or privileges of employment." This arguably broader language, the EEOC says, is evidence that more substantial adverse action is required to enable a plaintiff to prevail on a claim of discrimination than is required for a successful claim of retaliation. Retaliation will be found "if an employer retaliates against a worker for engaging in protected activity through threats, harassment in or out of the workplace, or any other adverse treatment that is reasonably likely to deter protected activity by that individual or other employees," according to the EEOC Compliance Manual.[56]

The EEOC's policy guidance permits its investigators to investigate any conduct that is "reasonably likely" to prevent employees from engaging in protected activity, regardless of the level of harm to the employees. This gives the EEOC investigatory authority that is broader and focuses on a wider array of conduct than would be found actionable by most courts. These issues, of course, are intensely factual determinations decided on a case-by-case basis, whether investigated by the EEOC or through litigation.

Post-Employment Retaliation

It is settled that retaliation may occur even after the employment relationship has ended. Post-employment retaliation is any action intended to interfere with a former employee's prospects for obtaining and maintaining employment. In 1997, the U.S. Supreme Court unanimously held that post-employment retaliation is actionable.[57] In that case, the plaintiff had filed an EEOC charge against his employer. The plaintiff argued that his former employer retaliated against him by giving him a negative job reference. The Court made it clear that unjustifiable negative job references can be the basis for retaliation claims, whether or not the former employee obtains employment elsewhere (for details, see Chapter 3).

Post-employment retaliation could also include refusing to provide a reference for a former employee.[58] This was the case in one dispute where a credit manager quit her job after failing to get a promotion she sought. The employee also stated that she planned to file a sexual discrimination claim against the company. A few months later, a representative of

---

[53] *Faragher v. City of Boca Raton*, 524 U.S. 775 (1998).

[54] EEOC Compliance Manual, §8-II(D)(3); *Knox v. State of Indiana*, 93 F.3d 1327 (7th Cir. 1996); *Passer v. American Chemical Society*, 935 F.2d 322 (D.C. Cir. 1991).

[55] EEOC Compliance Manual, §8-II(D)(3).

[56] *Id.*

[57] *Robinson v. Shell Oil Co.*, 519 U.S. 337 (1997).

[58] *EEOC v. L.B. Foster*, 123 F.3d 746 (3d Cir. 1997), *cert. denied*, 522 U.S. 1147 (1998).

another company requested a job reference for her. Although the employer routinely provided references for its former employees, it declined to do so in this instance. The former credit manager did not get the job she sought with the new company. The court held that the proximity in time of the credit manager's threat to sue, which was protected activity, to the company's refusal to provide a reference demonstrated a retaliatory motive.

It also should be noted that the actual effect of a negative reference or refusal to give a reference is completely irrelevant to the issue of whether an employer is liable for retaliation.[59] Any action undertaken to interfere with a former employee's prospects for employment may be considered retaliatory. This is true whether or not the actions prevent an individual from becoming employed. Thus, an employee who gets a new job, even though a former employer has given a negative reference or withheld a reference altogether, may still have a viable claim for retaliation. If the first employer's actions do not keep the former employee from obtaining employment, the plaintiff may be limited in the amount of damages or backpay available, but this will not relieve the employer of liability. Often, retaliatory discharge claims are combined with claims of post-employment retaliation.

Consequently, employers should take great care when giving references for employees who have engaged in protected activity. As with all employees, employers should take care to ensure that any information they provide is true. Additionally, employers should never provide information about an employee's protected activity. (Giving and obtaining references is discussed further in Chapter 4.)

Pre-Employment Protected Activity

A new employer's response to an employee's earlier protected activity with a former employer can also create liability.[60] One hospital learned this the hard way in its dealings with Anastasia Christopher, whom it had hired as a scrub nurse. Christopher previously had filed a sexual discrimination claim against the Wright State University School of Nursing while on its faculty. Christopher's new employer then had problems with her performance, finding that she lacked the necessary abilities, and was "disruptive" and "untrustworthy." She was removed from her position and she then sued the hospital for retaliation. The court found that Christopher's sexual discrimination claim against her former employer "had been mentioned enough times" by the doctors on the hospital's executive committee in reviewing her application for privileges to conclude that the hospital would not have made the same employment decision "absent the factor of the prior suit." Discussions concerning her prior claim and reference to it in a memo to the executive committee provided direct evidence of retaliation based on her prior sex discrimination suit. The court found that she had established a claim of retaliation.

Nexus Between Protected Activity and Adverse Action

Even if a plaintiff can show protected activity and adverse action, he or she must still prove that any negative or adverse action was related to or was taken because the plaintiff engaged in the protected activity. This can be proven through direct evidence or through circumstantial evidence. Direct evidence might include any written or verbal statement

---

[59] *EEOC v. L.B. Foster*, 123 F.3d 746 (3d Cir. 1997), *cert. denied*, 522 U.S. 1147 (1998); *Hashimoto v. Dalton*, 118 F.3d 671 (9th Cir. 1997).

[60] *Christopher v. Stouder Memorial Hosp.*, 936 F.2d 870 (6th Cir. 1991), *cert. denied*, 502 U.S. 1013 (1991).

indicating that adverse action was taken because an employee engaged in protected activity. For example, an employer's file may have a note stating that since an employee testified in legal proceedings against the employer, the employee's position will be eliminated in an upcoming reorganization. Or, as in *Merritt v. Dillard Paper Co.* (discussed earlier in this chapter), direct evidence was found in the company president's statement when firing the employee that the employee's deposition testimony in a sexual harassment suit had been the most damning evidence against the company.[61] Because direct evidence is not usually available, retaliation is more commonly proven through circumstantial evidence.

Circumstantial evidence does not come directly from an eyewitness or observer, or from actual documentation. It requires some reasoning or inference to prove a fact. In employment actions, circumstantial evidence may allow a trier of fact to infer that retaliatory animus motivated a negative or adverse action. For example, proximity of events in time can be considered as circumstantial evidence. When protected activity is followed soon after by adverse action, this is circumstantial evidence of retaliation, as shown in the following case.

An ultrasound technologist of Iranian descent was fired for unacceptable performance and because her employer believed she had stolen ultrasound films and a logbook.[62] The technologist denied the theft. The court said that because the investigation into the missing films and logbooks began within three months' of the filing of a discrimination complaint by the technologist, this timing could indicate a retaliatory motive.

Circumstantial evidence is often perceived by the general public as weak evidence. However, circumstantial evidence is often all that is available. The inference that can be made from circumstantial evidence may be so strong that there is very little doubt about an employer's intentions. This is especially true when an employer's stated reasons for taking an adverse action do not appear to be credible or justifiable.

Circumstantial evidence is more likely to be persuasive when adverse action follows very soon after the protected activity. However, longer intervals may still support an inference of retaliation when other factors are present. For example, an interval of 14 months was not too long when a pending EEOC charge was mentioned at least twice a week by the complainant's supervisor.[63]

Courts have also said that when an employer substantially changes its stated reasons for taking adverse action over time, this too can be viewed as circumstantial evidence of retaliation.[64]

Thus, it can be seen that the final element of a claim for retaliation — the causal connection — can be shown by direct evidence but is most often shown by circumstantial evidence. Once an employee or former employee has shown the requisite elements of a claim for retaliation, the employer has the burden of defending its actions.

---

[61] *Merritt v. Dillard Paper Co.*, 120 F.3d 1181 (11th Cir. 1997).

[62] *Hossaini v. Western Missouri Medical Center*, 97 F.3d 1085 (8th Cir. 1996).

[63] *Kachmar v. Sunguard Data Systems*, 109 F.3d 173 (3d Cir. 1997).

[64] *Kobrin v. University of Minn.*, 34 F.3d 698 (8th Cir. 1994).

▶ **Chapter 3: Defenses to Claims of Retaliation**

Employers may raise several possible defenses to a claim of retaliation. First and foremost, an employer should attempt to show that any adverse employment actions taken were based on sound, legitimate reasons, and were not taken in retaliation for protected activity. Documentation will be very helpful in this regard. Proof of legitimate, non-retaliatory reasons for taking disputed employment actions also will be helpful to an employer in establishing an "affirmative defense" or a "mixed motives" defense, as well as in defeating a plaintiff's claim of "pretext" (discussed later in this chapter). Insurance may be another way to limit liability.

First Line of Defense: Legitimate, Non-Retaliatory Justifications

Once a plaintiff has established the essential elements of a claim of retaliation, the burden then shifts to the defendant employer to state a legitimate, non-retaliatory reason for the action taken. This means that a plaintiff has established sufficient facts to state a case (referred to as the "prima facie case") and the employer must now respond. If an employer fails to respond at this point, the plaintiff wins the case. So to successfully defend itself against a complaint, an employer must respond by showing that it had a justifiable, legitimate reason for taking action against a plaintiff and that the action was not retaliatory.

In effect, this means that the defendant employer would have taken the same action regardless of the employee's participation in protected activity. Any truthful, justifiable and appropriate reason will meet this burden. For example, if an employee has been appropriately disciplined or discharged in accordance with company policies or practices, this usually will suffice as a defense. This brings home the crucial importance of documenting thoroughly any decision affecting employment, as well as having carefully delineated and disseminated corporate employment policies.

Justifiable, legitimate reasons employers might use to demonstrate non-retaliatory motives for employment actions include unacceptable performance, excessive absenteeism, violation of stated company policies or procedures, or serious disciplinary infractions. Again, the underlying employee behavior should be well-documented, and disciplinary actions should be taken only in accordance with company policies or past practices.

Former employees also may bring retaliation claims for negative references given by their former employers. In these cases, the truth of negative job references as well as compliance with the employer's own reference policies may serve as legitimate justifications for these post-employment actions and defeat the plaintiff's retaliation claims.

Evidence helpful in establishing the existence of justifiable, legitimate reasons for an adverse employment action could include:

- examples of similar disciplinary actions taken against other employees who have not engaged in protected activities;

- evidence of ongoing disciplinary procedures or performance concerns involving the complaining employee prior to his involvement in the protected activity; and

- the existence and enforcement of the same workplace rules or standards prior to the complaining employee's involvement in protected activity.

Some actions by an employee will be so serious that immediate dismissal is warranted, even when no previous warnings or evaluations support such action. One example of this would be violence by an employee. Although the risk of a claim of retaliation may be greater in a case where there is no record of prior warnings, it is still important to follow the course of action the employer would justifiably have taken had the employee not engaged in protected activity. It is especially helpful if an employer can provide evidence that it took the same type of action in similar instances with other employees who had not engaged in protected activity. If the situation has not occurred before but is serious enough to warrant immediate termination (as with an incident of violence), the employer should still proceed if it believes termination is justified. The fear of a potential claim of retaliation should not prevent the employer from maintaining its workplace in accordance with appropriate and important rules, especially those ensuring workplace safety.

In a number of cases, courts have found that employers charged with retaliation actually had justifiable, legitimate, non-retaliatory reasons for discharging employees. In one case, accountant Richard Jackson filed a complaint of reverse sex discrimination with the Equal Employment Opportunity Commission (EEOC) against the hospital that employed him.[1] He was later fired for inadequate and inefficient job performance, disruption of the workplace and harassment. The court ruled that discharging Jackson was proper because he had received "a long string of complaints and reprimands preceding his termination. The mere act of filing an EEOC complaint does not render illegal all subsequent disciplinary actions taken by the hospital . . . To require the hospital to overlook Jackson's past simply because he filed an EEOC complaint would unduly hamper the hospital's right to make employment decisions."

In another case, an employee had complained to management that she was being sexually harassed by her supervisor.[2] Subsequently, a co-worker reported that the employee had threatened to kill the company's human resource officer. The employee was fired pursuant to the company's "no tolerance" policy for threats of violence. The court said that the plaintiff employee had indeed engaged in protected activity (although the complained-of sexual harassment was not proven), but was discharged for a legitimate, non-retaliatory reason. The defendant employer's justification for termination was further supported because another employee (who had not engaged in protected activity) previously had been terminated for threatening a co-worker.

The courts tend to look favorably on employers who can document the legitimacy of adverse actions against employees who have engaged in protected activity. Employers should always have legitimate, justifiable reasons for taking adverse action against employees, whether or not they have engaged in protected activity.

---

[1] *Jackson v. St. Joseph State Hospital*, 840 F.2d 1387 (8th Cir. 1988).
[2] *Trumbull v. Century Marketing Corp.*, 12 F. Supp. 2d 683 (N.D. Ohio 1998).

Is the Employer Liable for Retaliation?

The following questions provide a framework for determining whether an employer might be liable for retaliation. (See flowchart on page 34.)

1. Did the employee ever complain to anyone about alleged discrimination or any other allegedly unlawful practice of an employer? (This could include, for instance, complaints of sexual harassment, improper payment of wages, or unsafe workplace conditions.)

2. If the answer to question 1 is "yes," was the complaint made reasonably and in good faith? (Illegal or unreasonable actions or complaints, or those not made in good faith, are not protected.)

or

Did the employee ever participate in any court or administrative investigation, hearing, or litigation relating to workplace conduct by filing a charge or acting as a witness or assisting in any other way?

If the answer to either of these questions is "yes," the employee has probably engaged in "protected activity" and may be protected from retaliation. Proceed to question 4.

If the answer to both of these questions is "no," proceed to question 3.

3. Is the employee closely related to or associated with any person who engaged in conduct described in question 1?

If the answer to question 3 is "yes," proceed to question 4.

If the answer to the first three questions is "no," the employer is not likely to be liable for retaliation.

4. Did the employer take any negative or adverse action against the employee?

This may include:
- refusing to hire an applicant;
- negative job evaluations;
- harassment;
- threats;
- increased observation or monitoring of the employee's performance;
- limiting or eliminating benefits, training opportunities or other workplace opportunities;
- demotion;
- discipline or discharge;
- providing negative references to prospective employers; or
- informing prospective employers about protected activity undertaken by the employee.

If the answer to question 4 is "yes," proceed to question 5.

If the answer to question 4 is "no," the employer is not likely to be liable for retaliation.

5. If the employer took any negative or adverse action against the employee, did the employer have legitimate reasons for doing so?

If the answer to question 5 is "yes," these reasons will be extremely important in defending against a claim of retaliation, and supporting documentation would be very helpful.

If the answer to question 5 is "no," the employer may face potential liability and should engage the best legal counsel available to address the employee's allegations.

Is The Employer Liable for Retaliation?

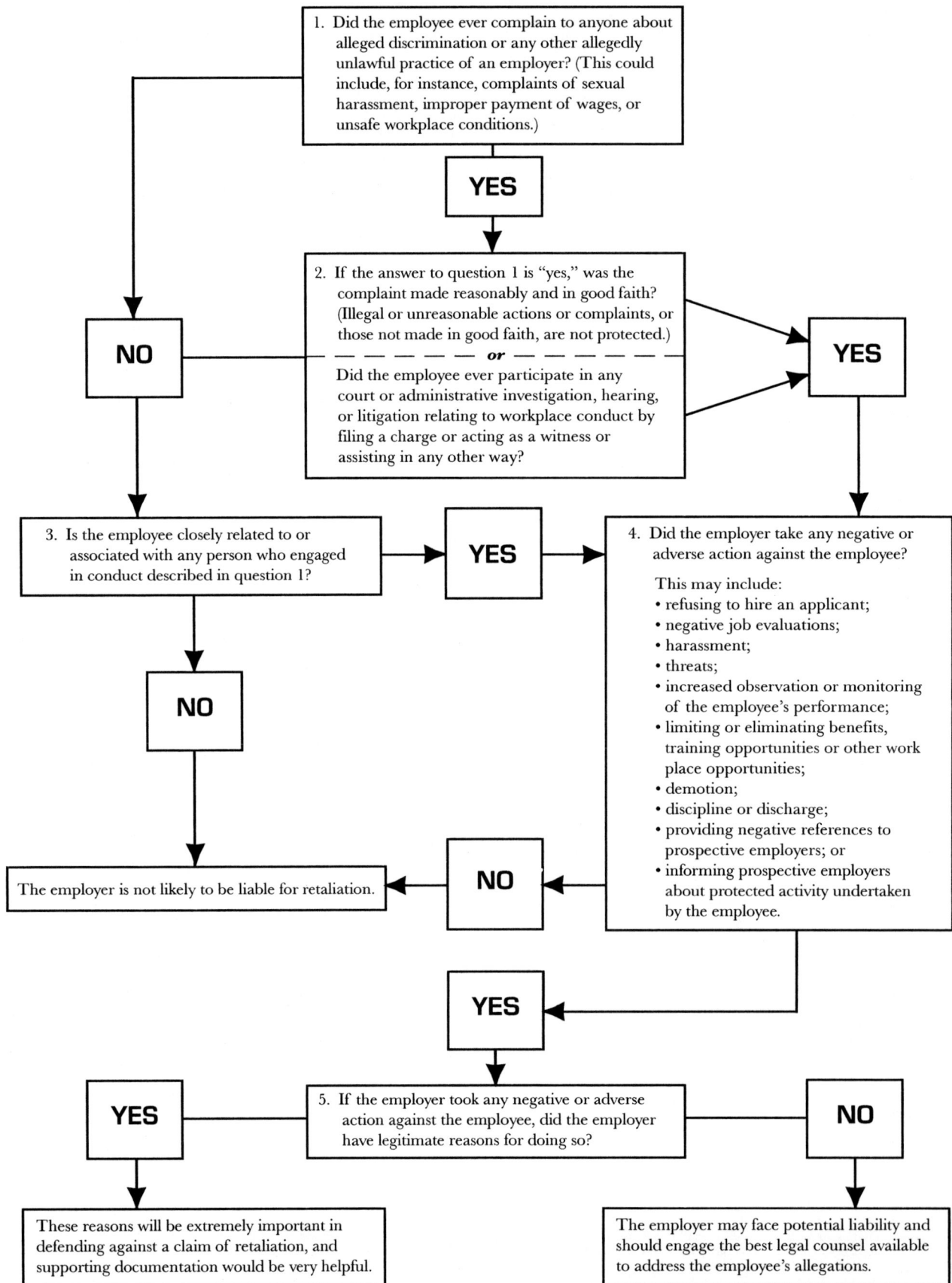

1. Did the employee ever complain to anyone about alleged discrimination or any other allegedly unlawful practice of an employer? (This could include, for instance, complaints of sexual harassment, improper payment of wages, or unsafe workplace conditions.)

YES

2. If the answer to question 1 is "yes," was the complaint made reasonably and in good faith? (Illegal or unreasonable actions or complaints, or those not made in good faith, are not protected.)

— — — — — — *or* — — — — — —

Did the employee ever participate in any court or administrative investigation, hearing, or litigation relating to workplace conduct by filing a charge or acting as a witness or assisting in any other way?

NO

YES

3. Is the employee closely related to or associated with any person who engaged in conduct described in question 1?

YES

4. Did the employer take any negative or adverse action against the employee?

This may include:
- refusing to hire an applicant;
- negative job evaluations;
- harassment;
- threats;
- increased observation or monitoring of the employee's performance;
- limiting or eliminating benefits, training opportunities or other work place opportunities;
- demotion;
- discipline or discharge;
- providing negative references to prospective employers; or
- informing prospective employers about protected activity undertaken by the employee.

NO

The employer is not likely to be liable for retaliation.

NO

YES

5. If the employer took any negative or adverse action against the employee, did the employer have legitimate reasons for doing so?

YES

NO

These reasons will be extremely important in defending against a claim of retaliation, and supporting documentation would be very helpful.

The employer may face potential liability and should engage the best legal counsel available to address the employee's allegations.

Affirmative Defenses

In 1998, the U.S. Supreme Court decided two significant cases interpreting federal law prohibiting sexual harassment.[3] In *Faragher v. City of Boca Raton* and *Burlington Industries v. Ellerth,* the Court held that employers may be held responsible for any sexual harassment by a supervisor in their employ that leads to a "tangible job consequence," such as a discharge or demotion. This is consistent with prior court rulings in *quid pro quo* cases in which a supervisor conditions an employment benefit upon an employee's acquiescence to the supervisor's sexual demands.

The Court added a new wrinkle though, stating that an employer also may be liable for a hostile environment created by a supervisor who had authority over the harassed employee even when the employer is unaware of the problem. Thus, an employer's potential liability was significantly expanded. An employer may raise an affirmative defense and reduce its liability in these circumstances, the Court noted, only *if no tangible employment action has been taken against the harassed worker.* To use the defense, the employer must be able to prove that 1) it exercised reasonable care to prevent and promptly correct any sexually harassing behavior; and 2) the complaining employee unreasonably failed to take advantage of any preventive or corrective opportunities provided by the employer "or to avoid harm otherwise," the Court said.

Courts also may apply this affirmative defense concept to retaliation claims. Many courts have used a variety of discrimination law principles in analyzing retaliation claims. Employers should ensure that they are in a position to take advantage of this possible affirmative defense.

With regard to the first requirement concerning reasonable care on the part of the employer to prevent and correct misbehavior, the materials set forth in Chapter Four of this book provide many suggestions that could be extremely helpful in establishing this element. Although the second requirement — that the plaintiff employee unreasonably failed to take advantage of any preventive or corrective opportunities afforded by the employer — is not wholly within the control of an employer, an employer at least has the opportunity to establish this affirmative defense by ensuring that it has appropriate preventive and corrective mechanisms in place for its employees.

Both of these rulings serve to stress the importance to employers of thorough training for supervisors and careful monitoring of the work environment.

Mixed Motives Defense

Employers often take adverse employment actions against their workers for several reasons, one of which may be legitimate, thus legal, and one of which may be retaliatory, and thus illegal. This is referred to as acting out of "mixed motives."

A "mixed motives" defense may be helpful to employers in defending against claims of retaliation. To establish such a defense, an employer must argue that even if it had acted illegally in taking adverse action against an employee in retaliation for participating in protected activity, the employer also had valid, legal reasons for taking the adverse action. For example, an employer might argue that even if an employee was discharged in retaliation for undertaking protected activity, legitimate business reasons also motivated the discharge. In other words, the defendant employer must argue that it would still have had legal and valid reasons to take the adverse action even absent the retaliatory motive.

---

[3] *Faragher v. City of Boca Raton,* 524 U.S. 775 (1998); *Burlington Industries v. Ellerth,* 524 U.S. 742 (1998).

For example, although an employee may have filed an earlier discrimination claim against an employer, the employee's excessive, well-documented absenteeism might be an appropriate, motivating factor leading to the employee's discharge. Retaliation may or could be an additional motivating factor.

Some courts have said that no claim for retaliation can be made where legitimate reasons support the need for adverse action and that these legitimate reasons provide a complete defense to liability, which relieves defendants from any obligation to pay damages.[4]

Other courts have held that establishing the existence of mixed motives merely limits the damages a defendant must pay to a successful plaintiff. According to the courts that have taken this position, the reasoning behind this is that if the plaintiff would have been fired for a legitimate reason completely apart from his or her involvement in protected activity, then the plaintiff was not damaged by the retaliation.

Recall that in *Merritt* (discussed in Chapter 1), the 11th U.S. Circuit Court of Appeals held that the employer was not liable for damages even though direct evidence of retaliation had been established.[5] Although Merritt may have had a valid retaliation claim based on his discharge (because his employer retaliated against him for his damaging deposition testimony), his employer still had a valid reason to discharge Merritt — his admitted sexual harassment of female employees. Thus, the court said that even if Merritt prevailed on his retaliation claim, he would not be entitled to damages because of the additional, valid and legal reasons for his discharge.

If a court allows a claim for retaliation where mixed motives are proven, employers will only be liable for declaratory relief (a judge's determination of the parties' rights under the law), injunctive relief, and attorney's fees. As in *Merritt,* no damages could be recovered nor would a plaintiff be entitled to reinstatement.[6] Whether a court considers the existence of mixed motives to be a complete defense to liability or merely to limit the type of damages available, it is extremely helpful for a defendant employer to be able to document the existence of all legitimate, non-retaliatory reasons or "motives" for adverse employment actions. Whenever the employer can show that it would have taken the same action against an employee, absent any retaliation, this will be a strong element of the employer's defense. Objective and well-documented evidence to justify discipline or discharge of an employee is crucial to defending a case and to establishing a mixed motives defense.

In fact, even evidence obtained about an employee *after* discharge may be helpful. In one case, a 62-year-old newspaper employee who had been with the company for 30 years was terminated as part of general cost-cutting measures.[7] She sued her employer, claiming that she had been let go because of her age. In the course of deposing her, the newspaper's lawyers learned that she had copied confidential documents during her final year of employment, conduct that would have resulted in her discharge if it had been discovered while she was an employee. The U.S. Supreme Court ruled that, where misconduct is discovered after termination, any backpay award will be limited to the date of the discovery of the misconduct.

---

[4] See, *e.g., Woodson v. Scott Paper Co.,* 109 F.3d 913 (3d Cir. 1997), *cert. denied,* 522 U.S. 914 (1997).

[5] *Merritt v. Dillard Paper Co.,* 120 F.3 1181 (11th Cir. 1997).

[6] §107 of the Civil Rights Act of 1991, 42 U.S.C. §§2000e-2(m) and 2000e-5(g)(2)(B).

[7] *McKennon v. Nashville Banner Publishing Co.,* 513 U.S. 352 (1995).

This "after-acquired evidence" doctrine provides that an employer may limit its liability to an employee who claims discriminatory discharge, if the employer learns, subsequent to the actual termination, that the employee engaged in misconduct warranting discharge while employed. This is true whether the discharge was originally motivated by retaliation (or discrimination) or not.

For example, assume an employee was fired in retaliation for engaging in protected activity. Two months after the unlawful discharge, the employer discovers that the employee embezzled funds from the company. Discharge at that time for the offense of embezzlement would have been lawful so the company can only be required to pay two months' worth of compensatory damages for the retaliatory discharge. Incriminating evidence discovered after discharge should be carefully documented, and may be useful in this regard.

Proving Pretext: the Plaintiff's Burden

Once a defendant employer has stated a justifiable, legitimate reason for taking adverse action with regard to an employee, the burden then shifts back to the plaintiff to try to show that the stated reason is merely a "pretext" for retaliation. A "pretext" is an excuse, alibi, or cover-up of the employer's real motives. It is very difficult for a plaintiff to show pretext once an employer has demonstrated the existence of a legitimate, justifiable reason.

A pretext exists when a purported legitimate reason is given to hide the true retaliatory motive for the action. A plaintiff can show pretext by showing that other similarly situated employees were treated more favorably than the plaintiff or that the plaintiff was treated more severely or strictly than other employees, after he or she engaged in protected activity. In a retaliation claim by a former employee, post-employment allegations of pretext may be proven if the employer deviated from its normal policy on providing references for former employees.

As stated, pretext is a difficult element of proof for plaintiffs to make. The pretext requirement forces a plaintiff to provide enough evidence to raise genuine doubt as to the legitimacy of the reasons provided by an employer defendant. The evidence does not need to directly contradict or disprove the defendant's reasons, it need only raise doubts. Also, a plaintiff can rely on the same evidence originally used to make a case of retaliation (the prima facie case) to show pretext. Types of evidence that can show pretext include evidence that the employer treated the plaintiff differently from other similarly situated employees, that the employee was more closely observed, or that the employer's reasons are simply not believable.[8]

At this writing, a case pending before the U.S. Supreme Court may require plaintiffs to prove even more to make a valid claim of pretext. The Court has agreed to consider the concept of "pretext plus" in an age discrimination case.[9] The issue before the court: What happens once an employer's explanation for allegedly discriminatory behavior is shown to be a pretext? Does the plaintiff then have a further burden to show direct evidence of the employer's intent to discriminate? This would be a difficult legal burden for plaintiffs to bear and is known as pretext plus. It could be extremely helpful to employers if plaintiffs are required to meet this additional burden.

---

[8] EEOC Compliance Manual, §8-11 E(2).
[9] *Reeves v. Sanderson Plumbing Products,* No. 99-536 (5th Cir. 1999).

Responding to a Charge of Retaliation

Once an employer receives an internal complaint of retaliation, it is probably best to seek the advice of qualified legal counsel. (For more information on the proper handling of complaints and investigating claims of retaliation, see Chapter 4.)

If an employer is sued or receives notice of any administrative action against the organization, contact legal counsel immediately. The time available in which to respond to a lawsuit or administrative action is governed by law and each day is critical. Do not delay.

The Role of Insurance in Limiting Liability

In response to a drastic increase in employment-related lawsuits, a growing number of insurance companies are now offering a special business coverage called Employment Practices Liability Insurance (EPLI). Until the late 1990s, this type of insurance was rare, offered by only a handful of insurers. However, as the number of workplace discrimination claims filed with the EEOC has continued to grow, with nearly 80,000 complaints filed in 1998, more companies have begun to demand insurance protection. EPLI policies are now offered by about 70 insurance companies nationwide, according to industry experts, and sales are growing at about 10 percent each month.

EPLI covers defense costs, judgments and settlements resulting from employment practices claims but may not cover punitive damages, fines or penalties assessed against an employer. Most EPLI policies contain a number of coverage exclusions, such as complaints alleging contractual liability, malicious intent or willful violation of the law. Prior to purchase, an employer should review an EPLI policy's description of coverage, exclusions and definitions to ensure that retaliation claims are specifically covered, particularly because they are a developing area of the law. Employers should always request clarification or representations about coverage in writing. Additionally, any liability covered by another policy, such as claims for workers' compensation, bodily injury or property damage, generally is excluded from EPLI coverage.

EPLI coverage usually encompasses the corporate entity and its directors, officers, employees and former employees, although some policies cover only managers and supervisors. Some policies also cover volunteers.

An organization can purchase coverage ranging from $1 million to $25 million, depending on the type of business and the degree of anticipated exposure. Most companies can expect to pay $75 to $100 per employee for coverage, according to industry sources. Although the available limits may seem generous, employers should remember that defense costs can quickly eat up their coverage. Defense costs generally comprise between one-third and one-half of all employment-related liability costs, so employers should consider defense expenses when calculating appropriate coverage limits.

Insurers assess several risk factors before agreeing to offer coverage. The underwriting process includes evaluating an organization's employee handbook, personnel policies and employment applications, as well as analyzing past insurance claims, allegations of employee misconduct and lawsuits. Insurers also pay close attention to the size of a company, the state in which it is located, the wages it pays, the ratio of male-to-female employees and the number of women holding executive positions. Industry sources say the EPLI underwriting process itself can be valuable because it entails such a comprehensive evaluation of an organization's existing employment practices.

One of the things insurers look for when reviewing applications for EPLI coverage is a strong working relationship between an organization's human resources department and its corporate attorneys. Insurers frequently use information solicited by an insurance application and questionnaire to determine an employer's philosophy regarding employment disputes.

Employers who don't have established workplace disciplinary procedures or guidelines may find themselves ineligible for EPLI coverage. Further, many insurers require their policy-holders to continuously train their employees to follow anti-discrimination laws. They also advise their policyholders to ask for help when they're unsure of what federal and state laws require. And, similar to car insurance, when too many claims are made, one of two things happens: either premiums go up or the insured entity is dropped.

Clearly, EPLI policies are not a cure-all and may not be substituted for good employment practices. When combined with solid personnel practices, however, EPLI can be an affordable and useful tool in alleviating employer concerns regarding liability. Because policy coverage and terms vary widely, employers should consider a number of factors before purchasing an EPLI policy, including:

- *Covered individuals.* Employers should pay particular attention to the inclusion or exclusion of specific individuals. The potential benefit of a policy is undermined if it doesn't cover the individuals ultimately named as defendants in a suit. In addition, companies going through mergers and acquisitions should consider whether a given EPLI policy will respond to claims arising from the target company's employment practices.

- *Scope of coverage and exclusions.* In addition to the common exclusions mentioned earlier, some policies exclude class action suits from coverage because they are expensive to litigate. Employers should note whether a policy covers class actions; if it does, the employer should examine the policy to determine how the deductible is to be applied. (Some policies have a per-claim deductible that applies once to a set of allegations while others have a per-claimant deductible that applies to each claimant even if the same circumstances are involved.) Employers should also check to see whether a policy excludes liability and/or defense costs incurred in administrative proceedings.

- *Liability limits.* Limits on the amount of liability covered by a policy may be on a per-claim basis, per-policy basis or both. Employers should assess their needs carefully when deciding on the appropriate coverage for their operations.

- *Deductibles.* The size of the deductible affects the cost of the policy premium. Deductibles in EPLI policies vary widely, so employers should compare the policies offered by various carriers before choosing one.

- *Coverage triggers.* Most EPLI policies specifically state when a claim is considered to be made and when it must be reported to them. EPLI policies usually are "claims made" policies, meaning that a claim is made when an employer receives written notice that an employee intends to hold it responsible for an alleged wrongful employment action. Most of these policies require the employer to immediately forward the claim to the insurer. "Claims made and reported" policies are slightly different in that they require that both events — the making and reporting of a claim — occur within the policy period. It is crucial for an employer to understand an insurer's requirements for processing a claim so that delays in payments or outright denials of coverage are avoided. If an EPLI policy is purchased, employers should take care to give prompt notice of any claim.

- *Overlapping coverage.* As noted earlier, EPLI policies usually contain "other insurance" clauses that exclude claims covered under more general insurance policies, such as workers' compensation claims. Before purchasing an EPLI policy, an employer should carefully examine these provisions to make sure it's clear how the EPLI policy will interrelate with potentially overlapping coverage provided by the employer's existing insurance policies.

- *Choice of counsel.* The costs of defending an employment suit using lawyers specializing in labor law are covered by any good EPLI policy. Most EPLI policies provide, however, that the insurer, rather than the employer, has the right to select defense counsel. These policies are known as "duty to defend" policies. If an employer has an established relationship with a particular employment lawyer whom it would like to use in the event of a lawsuit, the employer should raise this issue with the underwriter when applying for the policy. Policies that allow employers to select qualified counsel of their own choosing are known as "duty to indemnify" policies.

- *Loss control services.* A policy should offer an employer ongoing risk management, not simply risk transfer. For example, if an employer has to fire someone, it is helpful if it can receive advice on how best to avoid a legal problem or mitigate potential damage. An increasing number of insurers are offering this type of guidance as part of their services.

A well-crafted EPLI policy can be an effective shield against the risks of litigation, and the demand for EPLI coverage is likely to continue to grow as employment litigation risks increase. Employers should carefully assess their specific needs when considering whether to purchase a policy. Whether or not an employer chooses to purchase EPLI insurance, though, the bottom line remains the same: Proactive leadership by management is the best insurance against retaliation claims.

▶ Chapter 4: Preventing Retaliation

Retaliation may be more difficult for employers to guard against than discrimination or harassment. Retaliation can take so many forms that it is difficult to train employees and supervisors to recognize it and prevent it from occurring. It is a highly fact-specific matter. Employers should attempt to train employees and supervisors, however, so that they are aware of this potential claim.

The best defense against retaliation claims is the proverbial "good offense." A variety of preventive measures can help to protect employers from liability for retaliation before claims occur. Although nothing can prevent employers from being sued, many advance precautions can ensure that employers are ultimately successful in most litigation for retaliation.

Designing an Effective Retaliation Policy

Employers should of course have effective discrimination and harassment policies in place. These policies and related training should include express prohibitions against retaliation. As with harassment and discrimination, employers should establish a complaint procedure for retaliation claims. Internal complaint resolution is far preferable to litigation.

The retaliation policy can be a separate policy, but is probably most effective as part of a broader policy prohibiting discrimination and harassment. In either case, employers should make it clear that retaliation is prohibited and that offenders will be disciplined and possibly discharged. An employer with a strong retaliation policy will be in a better position to defend a claim of retaliation, and show that it took all possible preventive measures. (Sample policy language is included in Appendix D.)

An effective retaliation policy should contain:

- A statement that retaliation will not be tolerated in the workplace.

- A procedure telling employees how and to whom to make a complaint. Retaliation complaints can be brought to the attention of supervisors, human resources professionals or other managers. Experts advise against designating just one person to handle complaints to ensure that workers have a place to turn if the designated person is the offender.

- A statement that complaints will be investigated promptly and that appropriate actions will be taken against individuals found to have engaged in retaliation.

- A statement indicating that the employer will maintain information in as confidential a manner as possible. (*Note:* This does not mean employers can guarantee confidentiality — they cannot. Employers need to investigate complaints, and this usually necessitates telling those accused of retaliation the names of their accusers so they can properly defend themselves. For this reason, avoid promising *absolute* confidentiality.)

- A statement promising that the employer will not retaliate against an individual for lodging a complaint of discrimination or harassment nor allow any other employee of the company to engage in retaliatory behavior toward a complainant.

Effective communication of the policy statement to employees is essential. Employers should make sure all new and existing employees receive a copy of their organization's retaliation policy. To further ensure broad dissemination of its policy, an employer should:

- Post the policy on bulletin boards within each company facility;

- Include the policy in personnel manuals or employee handbooks;

- Discuss the policy at employee orientation meetings; and

- Discuss the policy during training programs.

Establishing a Complaint Procedure

An effective complaint procedure helps employers minimize or avoid liability. Employees who are aware of their organization's procedures usually are more inclined to file complaints or raise concerns within the organization than to turn to outside agencies or the courts. Further, employers may reduce their liability even when employees directly pursue external legal remedies if effective complaint procedures are in place and the employer has a track record of dealing effectively and fairly with employees.

Employers should make it easy for workers to bring forward complaints of retaliation. Employees should be assured that their complaints will be handled promptly and discreetly. They also should be reassured that managers will not permit retaliation to be taken against workers who file complaints.

These elements should be a part of any employer complaint procedure:

- Identification of supervisors, human resource officers or managers to whom complaint may be reported;

- Training for supervisors and managers on how to spot and report potential problems;

Tips for establishing a complaint procedure

In establishing a complaint procedure, it is helpful to keep these points in mind:

✓ The complaint procedure should permit employees to circumvent the normal chain of command when reporting retaliation.

✓ An employee's refusal to commit a complaint to writing does not excuse an employer from its responsibility to investigate the allegations. When complaints are made orally, the employer's representative should write down the complaint and, if possible, obtain the employee's verification that the prepared statement is accurate.

✓ The complaint procedure should be accessible and easy to use. If it is viewed as being too cumbersome, employees won't use it.

- Procedures for ensuring prompt investigations;

- Procedures for documenting complaints;

- Instructions for communicating with complainants;

- Instructions for maintaining confidentiality as much as possible; and

- Procedures for documenting the investigator's conclusions and recommended corrective action.

And finally, an employer must act immediately to stop retaliation. Failure to take prompt remedial action to address these problems may result in employer liability, so a prudent employer will implement a remedy reasonably likely to end the retaliation even before the investigation is concluded. Examples of swift remedial action include: offering the complainant or alleged offender a paid leave of absence for the duration of the investigation; or offering a temporary transfer to either of the parties, removing any offensive graffiti or materials from the workplace. (*Note:* Any leave of absence or job transfer offered during the investigation must not disadvantage either party or it may open the way to a suit against the employer.)

Investigating Complaints of Retaliation

The investigation of complaints of retaliation (or claims of harassment or discrimination) is extremely important. An objective and thorough investigation can greatly assist the employer in addressing workplace problems and may even provide a way to avoid liability.

In investigating any claims of retaliation (or of discrimination or harassment), employers must take care never to admit blame or liability. The actual terms "retaliation," "discrimination" and "harassment" should never be used by employers. These are legal terms with specific legal meanings. The employer's use of such terms could bolster a plaintiff's claim. If the employer itself documents "retaliation," it will be hard to argue before a jury at a later date that no retaliation occurred. The complained-of behavior should instead be referred to as "unacceptable," "offensive," or "inappropriate" behavior.

If an employer determines that it is likely that retaliation (or discrimination or harassment) occurred, this too must be carefully documented. Again, employers should not discipline an individual for "retaliation," "discrimination" or "harassment." The terms above, or similar terms, should instead be used. The employer should never create any documentation referring in any way to investigations or conclusions of workplace "retaliation," "discrimination" or "harassment."

Once an employee complains of retaliation, or any other allegedly unlawful act or practice, that employee must be protected from further retaliation. Whenever an employee engages in protected activity, employers must closely monitor the parties involved to ensure that no retaliation occurs. It is helpful to periodically confirm with the person who has engaged in the protected activity that retaliation has not occurred. If he or she reports that it has, this will enable an employer to act quickly to resolve the situation and end the retaliation.

It is understandable that supervisors and co-workers (especially those accused of improper behavior) would have difficulty continuing to work with the complaining employee. In many cases, supervisors and co-workers may even be fearful of the complaining employee. They may be reluctant to work together, fearing that they too may become the subject of a complaint.

However, care must be taken to ensure that the complaining employee can continue in his or her employment, without fear of retaliation. In cases where a complaining employee or disciplined employee will still be supervised or evaluated by an accused employee, employers should take care to review all employment decisions involving the complainant and monitor the supervisor's behavior toward the complainant. This will demonstrate the employer's commitment to avoiding retaliation and should reduce the likelihood of its occurrence. All involved supervisors and employees must be fully informed about their responsibility to guard against retaliation as well as the potential penalties if they engage in retaliatory behavior.

Unfortunately, in trying to respond appropriately to employee complaints, employers sometimes unintentionally retaliate. For example, if an employee complains of consistently offensive or discriminatory remarks by a customer, the employer may think the customer should be assigned to another employee. This would arguably resolve the issue for the employee (although depending on the nature of the remarks, the employer may also need to speak directly to the customer). However, if the customer's account generated large commissions for the employee, this may constitute an adverse or negative effect on the employee's compensation. This could form the basis for a claim of retaliation.

Steps for Handling Complaints

The following steps for handling complaints can be used to address claims of retaliation or discrimination in the workplace.

1. Immediately investigate all complaints, i.e., take all complaints seriously. Even if you feel sure a complaint has no merit, or if you believe that there has simply been a miscommunication, your duty as an employer is to investigate. You cannot simply ignore complaints. Further, an investigation shows that you take these matters seriously and it can help prevent liability. Employers may be liable whether or not they know about unlawful activity, so it is best to be fully informed.

2. Where possible, take complainant to a place where you can speak privately, free from interruptions.

3. Elicit as many facts as possible by asking the right questions, in a manner that does not place the victim on the defensive:

   - Name of person making complaint? Name of alleged perpetrator?

   - What happened? (Get specifics.)

   - When? (Date? Time?)

   - Where?

   - Name of persons involved?

   - Names of witnesses?

- Has this happened before? (If so, ask pertinent questions.)

- Have you made any notes about these incidents? (If so, ask for a copy.)

- What does the complainant want you to do about it? Please note that even if the complainant asks that you keep the complaint confidential or do nothing, a manager or supervisor has a responsibility to inform appropriate officers. Explain that the employer has an obligation to respond to all complaints and stop all retaliation, and that it wants to protect other workers from becoming victims of misconduct. Assure the complainant that the investigator and managers will only discuss the complaint with those who have a reasonable need to know about it.

- Is there anything else at all, or any other incident to report?

4. Have the victim submit a signed, written statement, preferably notarized. Confirm, in writing, that the statement is complete. Make sure the victim has included all incidents. This provides you with all relevant information and enables you to begin a thorough investigation. Also, if the victim leaves your employment and cannot be located, the statement is still available. Most importantly, once the victim has completed a notarized, written statement, which specifies that it evidences the *complete* complaint, it will be very difficult for the victim to embellish or change the story at a later date. Details of complainants' stories frequently change over the course of a lawsuit. A written statement made at the time of the complaint, which the complainant certifies as complete, can reduce the likelihood of this happening. (A sample complaint form appears in Appendix D.)

5. Take detailed notes of facts elicited during your meeting. Review your notes immediately after the meeting to clarify or correct them. Never use labels that refer to unlawful conduct, such as "retaliation" or "harassment." (See discussion earlier in this chapter, on investigating claims of retaliation.) One of the best defenses for an employer is to have the victim submit a written statement, signed and notarized. The victim should confirm in writing that the statement is complete.

6. Report the complaint to a human resources officer or other high-level member of management designated to handle these types of complaints.

7. Once a complaint has been made, it should be investigated by speaking with the alleged perpetrator and any witnesses, maintaining confidentiality to the extent possible. Employees who work directly with the involved parties should be questioned, as well as any likely witnesses. Even if a witness states that he or she has observed nothing, or has no knowledge of the allegations, this too can be extremely useful information and should be documented.

8. When questioning witnesses, be honest about your purpose. Ask that they maintain confidentiality. Ask open-ended questions to get the most information but verify details provided. Obtain all relevant information from each witness.

9. Review all available documentation. This will vary depending on the specific circumstances of the complaint, but could include an employee handbook or other rules and policies, personnel files of the parties involved, and any other documentation of prior complaints involving any of the parties.

10. Thoroughly document all aspects of the investigation. This documentation can be used to defend an employer if a complaint develops into a court case. Documentation should be comprehensive enough to show that an employer's investigation was thorough, fair and objective. Notes should be written clearly and be objective, factual and neutral. Documentation should include: the allegations of the complaint; the date the investigation started and concluded; the names of the investigators; a list of people interviewed and documents gathered; a summary of witness statements; a summary of the response from the person accused; the investigator's conclusion as to what happened, including an analysis of the parties' credibility; and a list of any applicable company policies. If an investigation is of a more minor nature, however, such in-depth documentation generally isn't necessary. A scaled-back version – an investigation summary in memo form for the investigative file, for instance – will suffice. (An actual example of thorough documentation is included in Appendix D.)

11. Take appropriate remedial action where warranted. Possible remedial action might include counseling, training, referral to an Employee Assistance Program (EAP) provider or rehabilitation.

12. Be consistent in your treatment of all complainants and alleged perpetrators.

13. Follow up with the complainant within the following six months to ensure that no repeat episodes have occurred. Employers often say that they "don't want to know," but the truth is they may be liable whether or not they know of continuing problems. If a problem is continuing, the employer can take additional, stronger action to put a stop to it. If the problem has not been repeated, the employer can document that the actions complained of have ceased. Either way, checking back in with the complainant can be extremely important in avoiding liability.

Remember, once an employee has filed a claim against the employer, or engaged in opposition activity, it is crucial to:

- consider all allegations of retaliation to be serious issues;

- investigate retaliation allegations promptly and thoroughly;

- follow standard policy and procedures, if possible; and

- conduct a thorough exit interview before termination as this may uncover a potential claim or provide a defense if the employer is later sued.

The Importance of Pre-Employment Screening

Measures designed to prevent retaliation can begin as early as the interviewing and hiring process. In addition, carefully measured responses are absolutely crucial when taking disciplinary action, particularly in discharging employees. In everything from checking references to maintaining personnel files to obtaining severance agreements, employers can take special care to avoid liability for retaliation.

Employers may wish to know whether prospective employees have ever sued their past employers. For example, a potential employer might find it extremely relevant to know that a prospective employee was involved in a race discrimination claim against a previous employer.

Employers often ask whether prospective employees have ever filed workers' compensation claims. As interesting and relevant as this information may seem, however, it is off-limits. The rationale for this prohibition is that employers would be less likely to hire a candidate who had previously sued an employer.

An employer should never ask job applicants or employees about litigation or complaints against previous employers. Any actions alleging discrimination or retaliation against former employers are considered "protected activity"; no other employer can use this as a basis for treating employees differently or for failing to hire job applicants (which is why it is referred to as "protected"). For this reason, application forms, interviews, reference checks and personnel files should never include this information. In fact, even if the information is volunteered, employers and prospective employers should completely disregard it. For example, if a reference for a prospective employee states that the employee sued his previous employer for discrimination, that information should not be recorded or disseminated. If an applicant states that she is pursuing a sexual harassment claim against her former supervisor, this too should be disregarded. Only job-related questions should be asked and recorded.

Asking only job-related questions can help demonstrate that an employer did not solicit information about protected activity and didn't act upon it. Application forms, lists of typical interview questions and lists of typical questions for reference checks can all help demonstrate an employer's objective hiring process. All employees and applicants should be treated fairly and consistently, whether or not an employer has information about protected activity. Such even-handed treatment can help an employer demonstrate that even an employee or applicant who has engaged in protected activity was treated consistently with all other employees.

Employees or applicants may sometimes need to request religious accommodations or accommodations for disabilities. These requests also should be disregarded in making employment decisions, regardless of how the accommodations were addressed.

Managers, supervisors, and others with interviewing or hiring responsibilities must be fully trained in what questions can and cannot be asked. Also, those in charge of maintaining personnel files must be aware of what information should and should not be maintained. Only job-related information should be solicited, retained or used in making employment decisions. Managers, supervisors, and others with interviewing or hiring responsibilities should be aware of what constitute appropriate and inappropriate questions and be familiar with the information guidelines on the following pages.

The following chart sets forth both lawful and unlawful questions and types of information solicited in application forms, job interviews, reference checks and personnel files. Anyone with interviewing, reference-checking or hiring responsibilities should know what information lawfully may be sought and what cannot. Additionally, those who maintain personnel files should be aware of the types of information that lawfully may be included and what may not.

Interview Questions

Topic	Lawful	Unlawful
1. Protected Activity	Why did you leave previous employment?	Have you ever filed a claim or lawsuit against any previous employer? Have you engaged in any past litigation, administrative actions and/or complaints against previous employers? *(Note: If the employee volunteers information regarding protected activity, disregard it and do not document it.)*
2. Name	Have you ever worked or studied under another name?	Inquiry into any title that indicates race, color, religion, sex, national origin, handicap, age or ancestry, or marital status. What was your maiden name? Has your name ever been legally changed? Do you want to be referred to as Miss, Ms. or Mrs.?
3. Address	Inquiry into place and length of residence at current or former address.	Inquiry into foreign addresses that would indicate national origin.
4. Age	Any inquiry limited to establishing that applicant meets any minimum requirements that may be established by law.	How old are you? What year did you graduate from high school? Requiring birth record before hiring is unlawful as is any other inquiry that might reveal whether applicant is at least 40 years of age, or over 70 years of age.
5. Birthplace or National Origin	Any inquiry into foreign language proficiency if job-related.	Any inquiry into place of birth. Any inquiry into place of birth of parents, grandparents or spouse. Any other inquiry into national origin.
6. Race or Color	None.	Any inquiry that would indicate race or color.
7. Sex/Gender	Gender, <u>only</u> if it is job-related (for example, to model women's clothes).	Any inquiry that would indicate sex. Any inquiry made of members of one sex, but not the other (for example, what will you do with your children while at work?)
8. Religion/Creed	None.	What religious holidays do you observe? Any inquiry that would indicate or identify denomination or custom. Applicant may not be told of any religious identity or preference of the employer. Employer can't request pastor's recommendation.
9. Citizenship	Whether legally authorized to work in the United States. Require proof of citizenship for I-9 after being hired. Whether an applicant speaks or writes English, if necessary for the job.	Whether native-born or naturalized. Proof of citizenship before hiring. Whether parents or spouse are native-born or naturalized.

Interview Questions

Topic	Lawful	Unlawful
10. Photographs	May be required after hiring for identification or security purposes.	Require photographs before hiring.
11. Arrests and Convictions	Inquiries into conviction of specific crimes related to qualifications for the job sought.	Any inquiry that would reveal arrest without conviction. In many states, any inquiry about conviction records that have been expunged.
12. Physical Condition	Any inquiry that is job-related (e.g., ability to lift 50-pound bags repeatedly with or without reasonable accommodation).	Any questions about height, weight, color of hair, skin or eyes. Will you need medical insurance? Any questions about necessary accommodations for disabilities.
13. Finances	Inquiry into personal finances if job-related (for example, a bank employee who will be evaluating customers' creditworthiness).	Any inquiry about bankruptcy, past garnishments, or home or car ownership (the EEOC states that these inquiries tend to discriminate against minorities). The Federal Bankruptcy Code prohibits employment discrimination based on the fact that a person has been bankrupt, a debtor in bankruptcy or is associated with someone who was bankrupt or a debtor in bankruptcy.
14. Education	Inquiry into nature and extent of academic, professional, or vocational training, if job-related. Inquiry into language skills, such as reading and writing of foreign languages.	Any inquiry that would reveal the nationality or religious affiliation of a school. Inquiry as to what is mother tongue or how foreign language ability was acquired. *(Note: The Supreme Court has said that asking whether an applicant has a high school diploma may be discriminatory, if not job-related.)*
15. Relatives	Inquiry into name, relationship, and address of person to be notified in case of any emergency. Inquiry into name and relationship of any relatives employed by the company.	Any inquiry about a relative that would be unlawful if made about the applicant.
16. Organizations	Inquiry into organization memberships and office held, excluding any organization, the name or character of which indicates the race, color, religion, sex, national origin, handicap, age or ancestry of its members.	Inquiry into all clubs and organizations where membership is held.
17. Military	Inquiry into service in U.S. Armed Forces. Require military discharge certificate after being hired.	Inquiry into military service of any country but U.S. Request for military service records. Inquiry into type of discharge.

Interview Questions

Topic	Lawful	Unlawful
18. Work Schedule	Inquiry into willingness to work required work schedule or anticipated overtime.	Any inquiry into willingness to work any particular religious holiday.
19. References	General personal and work references not relating to race, color, religion, sex, national origin, handicaps, age or ancestry, or protected activity.	Request references specifically from clergyman or any other person who might reflect race, religion, color, sex, national origin, handicap, age or ancestry of applicant, or protected activity.
20. Marital Status, Children, Pregnancy, Child Rearing Plans, Child Care Arrangements	None.	Any inquiry into these topics.
21. Transportation	Inquiry as to whether able to work required schedule, whether transportation is available. Any question regarding ability to travel, if job-related (e.g., whether applicant has a valid driver's license if position involves driving on company business).	Any inquiry into whether person owns a car, or as to specific transportation arrangements.
22. Disability/Handicap	Can you meet the attendance requirements of this job? Can you perform essential functions of the job with or without reasonable accommodation?	What current or past medical problems might limit your ability to do a job? Are you taking any prescription drugs? Have you ever filed a workers' compensation claim? How many days were you absent from your last job due to illness? Have you ever been a patient in a hospital? Have you ever been treated for drug abuse or alcoholism?
23. Sexual Orientation	(*Note:* Check local and state laws.)	(*Note:* Check local and state laws.)
24. Smoking	(*Note:* Check local and state laws.)	(*Note:* Check local and state laws.)
25. Relocation	Any inquiry about willingness to relocate, if required for the job.	Any inquiry about spouse's attitude toward relocation.
26. Other	Any questions required to reveal qualifications for the job applied for.	Any inquiry not related to job performance that may reveal information permitting unlawful discrimination, or retaliation.

All interview questions should be job-related. Prospective employers should never seek information regarding claims, actions or lawsuits against previous employers, or regarding any other form of protected activity by the applicant, such as requesting accommodations. The following suggestions can be helpful guidelines for all managers or supervisors with interviewing responsibilities.

Pre-Interview Preparation

- Formulate questions related to specific job requirements and follow this format for all interviews. Specific job-related inquiries are the most important and useful types of questions and will help avoid improper questions.

> ### Check Your Knowledge
>
> Decide whether each of the following interview questions is lawful or unlawful. (See answer key below.)
>
> 1. Do you own your own home?
> 2. Will the attendance requirements of the job be a problem for you?
> 3. Do you have young children in school?
> 4. Have you ever done this type of work before?
> 5. Shall I call you Ms. Brown or Mrs. Brown?
> 6. Have you ever been arrested?
> 7. Have you ever filed a complaint against a previous employer?
> 8. Will you be driving your own car to work?
> 9. How many sick days did you use in your last job?
> 10. Have you ever been convicted of a felony?

- *Always* ask why applicants are changing jobs. Investigate answers. If, however, an applicant volunteers that the change is due to litigation or a claim against a previous employer, this topic should not be pursued. Any such information should be disregarded.

- Consider carefully a change from a small company to a large one, e.g., structured vs. unstructured environment. Some employees will not successfully make these changes. Again, if the change is due to litigation or a claim against a previous employer, do not record this information. Do not consider it in making any decision.

- Always have applicants fill out *the employer's application forms,* even if you have their resumés. This is important because resumés provide information the applicant wishes to provide, not necessarily what you want or need. Further, resumés may include information about race, ethnicity, age, etc., that should not be circulated or considered in making employment

Answer Key
1. Unlawful.   (Refer to chart on pages 48-50, number 13.)
2. Lawful.   (Refer to chart, number 12 and number 18.)
3. Unlawful.   (Refer to chart, number 2 and number 4.)
4. Lawful.   (Refer to chart, number 26.)
5. Unlawful.   (Refer to chart, number 2.)
6. Unlawful.   (Refer to chart, number 11.)
7. Unlawful.   (Refer to chart, number 26.)
8. Unlawful.   (Refer to chart, number 13 and number 21.)
9. Unlawful.   (Refer to chart, number 1 and number 22.)
10. Lawful.   (Refer to chart, number 11.)

decisions. Finally, applications include certifications of truth and release language, as well as at-will statements. Resumés do not include this important language.

- Always have applicants fill out the forms in your office, especially for entry-level positions. This is a simple and easy way to test for basic literacy.

- Always ask whether an applicant is subject to a non-compete provision or other work-restricting agreement. This helps to avoid, or at least makes you aware of, potential litigation against the employee and/or you as the new employer.

Interviewing Techniques

Interviews usually reveal one thing very clearly — how well a person interviews. They do not necessarily reveal whether the applicant will be a successful employee. It is important to remember that if you make a mistake in hiring and have to fire someone within the first six months, the cost is high. One of the lowest estimates of cost is twice the salary for the position.

Most interviewers make up their minds in the first four minutes. This reflects the importance our culture places on first impressions. Unfortunately, the rest of the time is wasted as the interviewer merely works to confirm his or her opinion.

With these facts in mind, the interviewer's goal should be to talk only 20 percent of the time. The interviewee should talk most of the time. If the interviewer talks most of the time, the interview will not be particularly useful. The more *you* talk, the more you like the candidate (who has served as a good audience for you), but what will you have learned about whether the candidate will make a good employee?

You should expect short answers at first, because the interviewee may be nervous. However, simply waiting and encouraging the candidate to talk should achieve the desired results.

The following interviewing tips may help to elicit useful information:

- Use questions *sparingly*.

- Use verbal and non-verbal cues like "yes," "uh huh," and "I see," nodding and repeating the candidate's words to encourage them to continue.

- Don't rush to fill in gaps of silence.

Open-Ended Questions

Interview questions should be open-ended. Also, the best predictor of future success is past performance. Questions relating to actual past performance are better than hypotheticals because it is harder to make up answers. Be sure to ask for plenty of details. Some examples of open-ended questions dealing with past performance include:

- What led you to choose the college/major you chose?

- If you could relive your college/last ten years, what would you do differently?

- Can you give me an example of your ability to manage others?

- What are some of the things you have liked/disliked in past jobs?

- What was the most frustrating problem you encountered on a job?

- Tell me about your current/past job.

- Have you ever had to fire anyone? Tell me about it.

Self-Evaluation Questions

Self-evaluation questions are also useful in assessing potential candidates. Examples of these include:

- How would you describe yourself?

- Why do you think you are successful?

- Why do you think you got such good grades/were so successful?

- If I were to call your supervisor, what would she say about you? (This is a particularly good question because applicants know you may very well call.)

Do's and Don'ts in Interviewing

- Do encourage candidates to *think* before they answer — the longer, the better, as their answers are apt to be more relevant. Provide an environment in which thoughtful silence is not uncomfortable.

- Do *listen*. Don't be so concerned with formulating your next question that you miss the answers to your questions.

- Don't be afraid to *express concerns* with each candidate (don't wait until they're gone). In one interview for an executive director position, interviewers had discussed their concerns about the candidate's lack of previous supervisory experience. Their concern centered around whether she possessed the necessary leadership skills. When they expressed their concern during an interview, she shared information about her experiences as team captain and coach of various high school and college athletic teams, with ample examples of her leadership skills. This information was not in her resumé, and if the interviewers had not addressed it with her, they would not have had the benefit of this information. She was chosen for the position and was extremely successful.

- Don't sit behind your desk. This does not facilitate open communication.

- Don't think of the purpose of the interview as digging up dirt; help each candidate make the best case. This way you will be comparing all candidates at their best.

Value of Interview Notes

Notes are extremely helpful in the interview process. Carefully recording your perceptions and thoughts, as well as some of the candidate's answers, will assist you in making the best selection.

Because it is impossible to recall everything said in an interview, especially when considering multiple candidates, notes can help you recall important information. Both positive and negative notes should be recorded. This is especially true in areas where you are unsure or have doubts. Don't write so much, however, that you become distracted or distracting. In addition, never write on application forms or on resumés; keep your notes separate from these documents.

Immediately after an interview, review your notes and clarify or expand upon them as necessary. Then review and discuss any concerns you may have had about the interviewed candidate. Ideally, you will have addressed these concerns directly with the interviewee.

Notes can be discarded after a decision is made, but recordkeeping requirements do not permit the destruction of applications. In fact, applications are often maintained indefinitely as part of an employee's personnel file.

Interviewing Exercise

With the above mentioned guidelines in mind, develop answers to the following questions. After you have drawn up questions, use them with a partner or in small groups. See how much you can get them to talk, as you listen carefully and take appropriate notes.

1. Think of three questions that would be lawful, job-related and useful in an interview.

2. Think of three questions that are designed to get the most information from a prospective employee.

3. Think of three questions that would be lawful and useful on an application form.

4. Review your company's application form and identify any problems it contains.

Importance of References in Hiring

Checking references is a frustrating process for employers, yet it is one of the most important pieces of the hiring process. Former employers are often reluctant to share information because of fear of a possible defamation claim if negative information is provided. However, the truth of the information provided (whether negative or not) is almost always a complete defense to a claim of defamation. Also, most states have enacted statutes offering protection from liability for employers who give references in good faith. And in fact, employers can even be sued for a false reference or references that don't fully disclose pertinent information.

One example of this involves an employee who was fired from his job at Allstate Insurance Company for carrying a gun to work and threatening co-workers. Yet, the company's letter of reference claimed he was ousted because of "corporate restructuring." He had even received a four-month severance package. The employee landed a job at Firemen's Fund, subsequently lost the job and then gunned down three Firemen's Fund executives as they ate lunch at a cafe. Family members sued Allstate over the misleading reference and garnered an undisclosed settlement.[1]

In another case, two school districts gave glowing recommendations to a former vice principal without disclosing that he had been charged with sexual misconduct and impropriety. Those letters persuaded another school district to hire the man, who later sexually assaulted a student. The family of the student sued the former employers over negligent misrepresentation and fraud, and the California Supreme Court held them liable.[2]

However, employers may provide negative job references in any situation, as long as they are truthful. In addition, to avoid a claim of retaliation, even a truthful negative evaluation must not be a "pretext." In other words, a truthful negative evaluation may not be a disguise for retaliation. This could be the case in a situation where an employer's policy is that no

---

[1] *Jurner v. Allstate Insurance Company*, Civ. No. 09472 (Fla. Cir. Ct. 1995).
[2] *Randi W. v. Muroc Joint Unified School District*, 929 P.2d 582 (Cal. 1997).

reference information, or only minimal information, is given for past employees. However, if the employer makes an exception, in contravention of its policy, and provides negative (even though truthful) information regarding an employee who has engaged in protected activity, this could be a pretext for discrimination. Truth would not be a complete defense in that situation.

One area of exception to truth as a defense results from the laws prohibiting retaliation. If an employer provides information that an employee has engaged in protected activity, the employer may be liable for retaliation, even if the employee still gets the job.[3] The safest course of action is to provide only truthful, objective, job-related information. Information about an employee's participation in protected activity should never be shared with prospective employers or others seeking references.

In another case involving references, Phillips School of Business and Technology was asked for a reference for a former employee, Otha Lee Fields. Fields had been terminated by the school and subsequently had filed a charge of race discrimination against the school under Title VII. The school completed a standard reference form from the prospective employer, checking boxes indicating that Fields was "below average" in several categories and that she was terminated due to tardiness and insubordination. The school made no reference to Fields' Title VII charges. The court held that because the school relied on personal observations and its business records in completing the form, no malice or ill will on the part of the school was demonstrated, and no claim for retaliation could be made.[4] This case shows how providing truthful, documented information (and not providing information about protected activity) in response to a request for a reference can be effective and safe for employers.

Of course, when you are seeking references, you want to obtain as much information as possible. Even though you cannot ask about past or current protected activity, much information can be gathered through a thorough, diligent reference process. Creativity is also useful. Some creative questions might include the following:

- "Would you rehire this person?"

- "I know you can't answer [a given question], but if you could, what would you say?"

- "I'd really like to consider this person for a job, but I can't because I'm concerned that there must be something negative in their work history if you can't share any information."

Try Different Routes for References

When contacting current or past employers, contact the supervisor, not the human resources department (request the supervisor's name on your application). Typically, only human resources personnel are familiar with their company's policy on giving references; contacting a supervisor may yield more information.

In contacting supervisors for references, the higher up the chain, the better. Senior officers are often unaware or unconcerned with reference policies and consequently are more likely to provide information.

---

[3] *Robinson v. Shell*, 519 U.S. 337 (1997).

[4] *Fields v. Phillips School of Business and Technology*, 870 F. Supp. 149 (W.D. Tex. 1994), *aff'd mem.*, 59 F.3d 1242 (5th Cir. 1994).

Attempt to get references from references. Ask each reference that the prospective employee has provided for at least one additional reference. These people may be quite knowledgeable about the candidate and more apt to provide information. They are not anticipating your call and may be quite open and honest.

Tips on Giving References

1. Establish a clear policy on how to provide information to other employers, identifying those employees authorized to release information. No matter what the policy, all employees must be aware of it and abide by it. Supervisors who are unaware of the policy or who do not understand the importance of a reference policy can create big problems for employers.

2. Be consistent with the type of information conveyed. If an employer's policy only allows disclosure of dates of employment, final position and salary, make sure that *no* other information is provided. Giving additional information for "good" employees creates by implication a more negative reference when only minimal information is provided for other employees.

3. Make sure you know whom you are speaking to and that it is someone with a legitimate right to know. Ask for reference requests in writing on company letterhead or take a telephone number and call back. Do not simply respond to phone calls from an unknown person. Potential plaintiffs quite often engage a third party to pose as a prospective employer to see if negative information is provided. A Houston insurance agent hired a private investigator who was told by the agent's former employer that he was a "classic sociopath," a "zero" and that he lacked scruples. Of course, none of this was or could have been documented objectively. The former employee was awarded $1.9 million by a jury.

4. Keep a written record of who gives references, to whom and when.

5. Give references only if the employee in question has provided a written release. Note that in many cases, the Fair Credit Reporting Act requires a separate, specific release. Check with counsel to see if this law applies. (*Note:* The act's provisions are not limited only to credit checks.)

6. Convey only job-related information, preferably that which has been documented.

7. Make sure the information is factual and objective.

8. Don't be malicious.

9. Answer questions but don't volunteer opinions. Remember, "off the record" is a media concept, not one that is applicable in this context.

10. Whenever possible, put the reference in writing to help maintain control over what is communicated.

11. If the request concerns a former employee involved in a claim or litigation against the company or a former employee whom you think may be dangerous, talk with your attorney about what to say and how to say it.

Personnel Files: What to Keep?

Those employees in charge of maintaining personnel files should be careful to ensure that no unlawful information is included in the files. In terms of retaliation, this means that any information about protected activity should not be included in an employee's personnel file. Some examples of protected activity information that should not be maintained in a personnel file include the following:

- Equal Employment Opportunity Commission (EEOC) or other administrative agency documentation of a charge filed by the employee;

- copies of a subpoena by a court or administrative agency;

- investigative documentation of complaints of unlawful activity in the workplace;

- workers' compensation claim records;

- requests for religious accommodation; and

- requests for accommodation of disabilities.

This is not to suggest that this type of information should not be maintained, but only that it be maintained separately from personnel files.

The reason for excluding this information from personnel files is that in making employment decisions (such as assessing qualifications for promotion, conducting periodic evaluations, providing training opportunities, or administering discipline), presumably the decision-makers refer to personnel files. Therefore, the files should not include any information that would be unlawful to use in making employment decisions, including information on an employee's participation in protected activity, race, disabilities, etc. (For a more detailed discussion of unlawful information, see material on the importance of pre-employment screening earlier in this chapter.) Keeping this type of information separate from personnel files helps to show that decision makers didn't take it into account, specifically in reaching negative employment decisions. Conversely, if unlawful information is included in the file, it will be presumed to have been taken into account in making a negative decision. This will assist a plaintiff in developing circumstantial evidence to show that an employer's justification for taking action was merely a pretext for retaliation or discrimination (as discussed in Chapter 2).

Too often, employers seem to believe that personnel files are actually kept for the benefit of employees. For example, employers may think that an employee's file should be a complete record of employment carefully maintained by the employer for the benefit of the employee. Employers often keep every document regarding every employee. This is actually the opposite of what an employer's goal should be. Employers should consider personnel files to be carefully maintained *company* records, kept for the sole and exclusive benefit of the employer. They should be as carefully maintained and safeguarded as financial information, tax records, or any confidential or trade secret information. Access should be limited and files should be locked. Properly maintained personnel files can be extremely helpful in litigation. Overinclusive files can be devastating.

The following list is a summary of what personnel files should and should not include. Several items require explanation. Again, keep in mind that the items on the "Should Not Include" side of the list may be maintained by the employer, but not in the personnel file.

Employee Personnel Files

Should Include	Should Not Include
• Signed employment contract or signed handbook receipt	• I-9
• Employment application (resumés)	• Self-Evaluation Forms or "Responses" to Performance Evaluations
• Performance evaluations or reviews (recommend no more than two most recent)	• Medical records (including any related to the Americans with Disabilities Act and including any documentation of absences for medical reasons which may constitute disabilities)
• Disciplinary warning notices	
• Absence, tardy, and vacation records (documentation for non-medical leaves of absences and documentation that does not evidence protected activity)	• Health insurance records
	• Records of achievements, honors, community service
• Signed Code of Ethics (if applicable)	• Letters of praise or commendation from customers or other third parties
• Current mailing address and phone number	
• Employee status (part-time, temporary, or full-time)	• Workers' compensation records
	• Investigative consumer credit reports
• Emergency contacts	• Any information that could be viewed as the basis for discrimination
• Job information - promotion, demotion, layoff, transfer, bids - seniority - training and education	• EEO/Affirmative Action records - Post-hire information - Declaration of disability - Complaints of discrimination and investigation material
• Fingerprints (if necessary, e.g., for security)	
• Photographs (only if necessary, e.g., for security)	• Requests for religious accommodation
	• FMLA request forms and related forms
• Payroll information	• Requests for accommodations for disabilities
• Certificates or licenses required for the job (e.g., valid drivers license for drivers)	• Documentation for absences due to "participation" in any investigation, hearing or litigation of a charge of discrimination or other illegal practices
• Exit interview	
• Termination report	• Any other evidence of "protected activity"

Most employers maintain performance evaluations or reviews in personnel files, but note that the list states that no more than two should be maintained. Most employers keep these documents indefinitely, so that an employee employed for ten years may have ten or more evaluations. This is never helpful and can be extremely harmful.

An example can demonstrate the problem. Suppose an employee has been fired for poor performance and claims that the real reason was retaliation for filing a claim of race discrimination. The personnel file is requested by either the EEOC (or state administrative agency) or by the plaintiff's attorney in litigation. It includes the past six years of performance evaluations. Supervisors are generally reluctant to properly document poor performance, or to be too critical. Therefore, the five earliest performance reviews show average performance, which is also the rating a poor performer is most likely to receive. "Average," in a juror's mind, or the mind of an agency investigator, is not substandard. So it might appear that the only "bad" performance review was the final one, which also came after the employee complained of race discrimination. Even if the employee's performance was substandard, this will be good circumstantial evidence for the employee. The employee or the employee's attorney will argue that the employee's performance reviews were fine, year after year, until the employee complained of the discrimination.

What if, in fact, the employee's performance was consistently bad throughout the years, even before the claim of race discrimination? And what if that poor performance was properly documented? Then, wouldn't it be helpful to show that for six years the employee performed poorly and documentation of this did not change after the race discrimination charge? In this case too, maintaining all these evaluations would be harmful rather than helpful. If it is true that the employee was a consistently poor performer for all six years, why then was the employee fired only after complaining of race discrimination?

As has been demonstrated, large numbers of performance evaluations are never helpful. Two prior evaluations are the most that should be maintained; one is actually sufficient and preferable. Also, if managers track performance and document whether a prior performance or disciplinary issue has been resolved, this will provide ample "history" for the next review period. Personnel files should all be purged of excess performance evaluations. The one exception to this arises where an employer knows or is reasonably sure that an employee has filed or intends to file a charge or lawsuit against the employer. In this case, no documentation concerning that employee should be destroyed or deleted.

Also, employee self-evaluations or "responses" to performance evaluations should not be included in personnel files. This is evidence that may be helpful to employees in disputing negative performance evaluations. Self-evaluations can be useful in the performance review process, but should not be maintained by the company. They may support an employee's case against the employer and maintaining them in company files gives them a presumption of credibility. Employees often want to respond to performance evaluations, especially those that are critical. Employees may wish to write notes to their files; some performance evaluation forms even include a section for an employee response. If an employee has "explained," justified or disagreed with an evaluation, maintaining that documentation in the company's personnel files only strengthens the employee's case and weakens the employer's.

Of course, attendance records are appropriately maintained in personnel files. However, care must be taken to remove documentation of reasons for absences that include unlawful information. Examples of this type of documentation would include medical records or doctors' excuses that refer to disabilities or records of requests for days off for religious observances. In terms of retaliation, subpoenas for witnesses in discrimination or other proceedings against an employer would also be unlawful information.

Two other items on the following list require some explanation. Note that "records of achievements, honors, community service" and "letters of praise or commendation from customers or other third parties" are included on the list of items that should not be included in personnel files. This often comes as a surprise to employers. However, once an employer understands that personnel files are company records, for the sole and exclusive benefit of the employer, the rationale becomes clear.

You can imagine the impact on a jury of a personnel file that includes several glowing letters from customers and various awards for charitable work. The employer wants to argue that the employee was fired for poor performance or for disciplinary problems. The employee wants the jury to believe that the employer's stated reasons are not true (see discussion of pretext in Chapter 2). The employer actually provides its own company records, which show that the employee is loved by customers and is a good person. The employer is placed in the position of actually supporting the employee's case against it with its own company records. This is obviously not the intended purpose or desired effect of personnel files.

When employees receive honors, awards and favorable letters from customers, these are occasions for which employees deserve recognition. The employer wants its employees to be recognized in these ways. Simple words of acknowledgment, posting the items on the company's bulletin board or web site, or writing about these items in the company newsletter are just a few ways in which to recognize deserving employees. The awards, letters and other documentation can then be given to the employee.

If the employee saves and later uses these documents to support a claim against the employer, they will be far less helpful to the employee. A jury or judge will expect the employee to provide self-serving support for his or her claim. This will be far less damaging than if the employer maintains the documentation as part of its official company records, especially those that are specifically used in making employment decisions. In fact, the employer's records are given special status as evidence because of a presumption of reliability and authority. Those records should never provide any support for an employee's claim against an employer.

If an employer decides to remove materials from personnel files, it must do so consistently. In other words, if you decide to maintain only one performance evaluation, remove all others from all employees' files. Do not maintain additional performance evaluations for a particularly bad employee, for example. Also, once documents are removed, they should be destroyed. Storing them offsite in cardboard boxes still means that they are maintained as company records. Most importantly, when purging or removing any records from personnel files, never remove or destroy anything from an employee's file if that employee has filed a charge or complaint against you, or if you have reason to believe that will occur. (See Appendix D for a sample personnel file.)

Disciplining Employees After Protected Activity

"Aren't employees 'at-will'?" an employer might ask. "Doesn't our company handbook say that they can be fired at any time, for any reason or for no reason?" Most states have at least some at-will employment protection for employers. At-will employment means that employees or employers may terminate employment, at any time, with or without cause or notice. Some exceptions to this doctrine exist, however, and the doctrine never permits unlawful retaliatory discharge or discriminatory discharge. To maintain the protection of the at-will doctrine to the extent possible, at-will language should be included in bold or capitalized language in application forms, handbooks and other documents provided to applicants and employees.

Even when employers have taken all precautions to protect the at-will status of employees, retaliatory discharge is still prohibited. Exceptions will be made to the at-will doctrine to prevent retaliation regardless of the reason for discharge.

This can lead to surprising results. For instance, one court has held that a pharmacist could not be fired even though his pharmacist license had expired. The pharmacist had been told that he was being fired because his license had expired. However, he had recently complained to his employer (and threatened to complain to the FDA) about improperly stored drugs in the pharmacy where he worked. He argued that he was fired in retaliation for his complaints. The court held that the employee's complaints and threats created a "public policy" exception to the District of Columbia's employment-at-will doctrine. The court held that if internal complaints such as this one were not protected, this would "create perverse incentives" to avoid reporting problems. An employee would be forced to choose between continuing to work for an employer that is violating the law or losing his or her job. This is a choice that employees should not have to make, said the court.[5] Employers should always carefully justify and document legitimate reasons for discipline and discharge to avoid a similar situation.

Employees who have engaged in protected activity may still need to be disciplined or discharged. Sometimes the reason for discipline or discharge will become apparent as a result of participation in protected activity. For example, an employee might admit to some illegal activity while testifying in a court proceeding, as in *Merritt v. Dillard* (see discussion in Chapter 2). The employer might then have a legitimate basis for discipline or discharge, but the employee would be protected from retaliation.

How can employers avoid liability in these situations? In addition to following the general guidelines for disciplining or discharging employees (see discussion of corrective discipline later in this chapter), employers should take these additional precautions when considering discipline or discharge of employees who have engaged in protected activity:

- Ensure that any discipline or discharge is not based on the employee's protected activity.

- In communicating with the employee, make it clear that the discipline or discharge is based on the misconduct or unacceptable performance.

- Carefully document the reasons for the discipline or discharge, as well as all communications with the employee.

- Have a witness who can verify what was communicated to the employee and who can also document the conversation with the employee.

In disciplining employees, care should be taken to do so fairly to minimize or avoid any potential claims an employee might have, especially potential retaliation claims. Employers should strive for consistency, treating similar situations similarly. Performance objectives

---

[5] *Liberator v. Melville Corp.*, 14 IER Cases 1545 (D.C. Cir. March 16, 1999).

should be communicated clearly to employees. Employers should give and document feedback and provide constructive criticism. Employees must have knowledge of rules and warnings so they can make a full effort to comply with them.

Carefully document all employment decisions involving adverse actions, especially discipline and discharge situations. Attempt to treat all employees fairly and in the same way, regardless of whether they have engaged in protected activity. Never take any adverse action, or discipline or discharge an employee (or fail to hire an applicant) simply because he or she has engaged in protected activity. Document all disciplinary incidents and unacceptable performance. This will provide evidence of the employer's justifiable, legitimate reasons for taking adverse action against an employee. Proper documentation can refute the

---

Positive Steps to Corrective Discipline

1. Get all the facts in each and every disciplinary investigation. Don't assume anything is true. Be as fair and objective in an investigation as possible.

2. Check past practice and act consistently.

3. Determine what step or stage of the disciplinary progression the employee is within and follow the prescribed steps exactly, if applicable.

4. Perform the disciplinary action in private.

5. Avoid distractions and interruptions.

6. Specify the reasons for the actions taken. Don't be vague.

7. Get the employee's side of the story directly from the employee, and determine if there are any mitigating or compounding circumstances that could affect your preliminary decision.

8. Try to determine whether the employee's behavior calls for some form of assistance or rehabilitation, rather than discipline.

9. Establish future consequences. In doing this, the language should always include the words, "further discipline, up to and including termination."

10. Carefully document the reason for discipline and explain future consequences that can be anticipated if performance does not improve. If further discipline or discharge is a possible consequence, make that clear to the employee. Even "verbal" warnings or reprimands should be documented in an employee's personnel file.

11. Follow up with the employee as to continuing problems or improvements in performance.

12. If discharge is necessary, the employee should be discharged with dignity. Don't be vague. Give guidance on what happens next. Don't give the employee false hope that a decision may be reversed. The employee may have to go home and face a spouse or family who will have many questions. Try to give the employee as much information as possible about such things as continuation of health care coverage, manner and timing of final pay, etc. The chance that an employer will be sued depends largely on how the discharge is handled and the employee's ability to find a new job. The employer is in complete control of the former, and should do its best to help the terminated employee preserve his or her dignity.

---

employee's claim that the adverse action was retaliatory. This is always good practice but becomes especially important when taking adverse action against employees who have engaged in protected activity.

When discipline is required, employers must be sure that it is reasonable. Employers should consider the nature of the offense, the employee's prior employment history, and whether the "punishment fits the crime." Some conduct is so serious or extreme that immediate discharge is the only solution. Applicable policies must be considered, as well as past practice in similar situations. If a formal, progressive disciplinary policy exists, the employer should follow it to the letter.

When disciplinary action is warranted or when poor performance needs to be addressed soon after participation in a protected activity, employers become especially concerned about potential liability for retaliation. Management may be reluctant to address these important issues for fear of a claim of retaliation. Do not delay justifiable adverse action. Be aware of the timing of the adverse action in relation to the protected activity, but don't necessarily change it.

While precautions can never ensure that an employer won't be sued, important actions can be taken to avoid liability. As always, fair and consistent disciplinary practices will go a long way in protecting employers from all types of employment claims, not just retaliation claims. Certain procedures should always be followed — even in at-will employment states where employees and employers theoretically can terminate employment at any time with or without reason or notice — and are especially important in avoiding potential retaliation claims.

The Effect of Severance Agreements and Releases

Employers often obtain releases of liability or severance agreements from departing employees as another avenue to avoiding liability for any possible employment claims. The purpose of these releases or agreements is to give some benefit to the departing employee in return for the employee's agreement not to sue the employer. This promise not to sue can encompass all potential claims of discrimination or retaliation. Consequently, this is a good preventive measure and, when entered into after consultation with legal counsel, can help avoid lawsuits by employees.

Several important legal issues are involved in any attempt to get a release, so legal counsel should always be consulted. No release or severance agreement should be used unless it has been drafted or approved by counsel.

An additional problem arises concerning retaliation. The EEOC and several courts have said that no release or severance agreement is effective in prohibiting an employee or former employee from filing a charge with the EEOC or from assisting or participating in an EEOC investigation. In other words, even though an employer has paid money or provided some additional benefit to an employee in excess of what the employee may have been entitled to under company policy or procedures and the employee has agreed not to sue the company, the employee may still bring an EEOC charge against the employer, even on the very same issues for which the employee released the employer from liability.

This result may seem surprising, but several points should be considered. First, the EEOC acts in large part to protect not only private parties, but also the public interest and national policy favoring the prevention of employment discrimination. If certain individuals were prevented from assisting the EEOC, the EEOC's mission would be thwarted in many cases.

Second, these releases and severance agreements would have a chilling effect on employees' willingness or ability to provide the EEOC with information. And finally, under both Title VII of the Civil Rights Act and the Americans with Disabilities Act (ADA), the EEOC may not begin any investigation without at least one actual individual charge. (Under the Age Discrimination in Employment Act (ADEA) and the Equal Pay Act (EPA), however, the EEOC may investigate without a charge.)

Employers might be asking why they should pay money or provide a benefit to obtain a release when employees can still sue. One very good reason remains. Even though an employee would not be prevented from filing an EEOC charge, an employee would be prevented from recovering any additional money or benefit from the employer. In other words, an employee may not waive the right to file a charge with the EEOC but may waive the right to any recovery in such a proceeding.

Careful drafting can accomplish this necessary balance. For example, the following sample language achieves this balance:

> Employee releases the Company, its affiliates and any successors, directors, employees, agents, and assigns from any and all claims, actions, causes of action, claims for relief, damages and demands which Employee now has or may have against the released parties arising out of employment or the termination of employment, including any possible claims, rights or causes of action arising under the Age Discrimination in Employment Act or the Older Workers Benefit Protection Act, any other claim of discrimination on any basis, any contract claim or any claim of defamation. Employee agrees not to prosecute or pursue any claim against the Company that this Release purports to cover. Notwithstanding the foregoing or any other provision of this Agreement, this Release is not intended to interfere with Employee's right to file a charge with the Equal Employment Opportunity Commission ("EEOC") in connection with any claim Employee may have. However, by executing this Agreement, Employee waives the right to any recovery in any such proceeding, or in any state civil rights commission proceeding, or in any proceeding brought by the EEOC or any state civil rights commission on Employee's behalf. This Release is a release of both known and unknown claims. This Release does not extinguish any rights or obligations arising under this Agreement. The Company expressly denies any liability or alleged violation. Payment is made pursuant to this Agreement solely for the purpose of compromising any and all claims without the cost and burden of litigation.

This contractual language and any additional release language should be drafted or carefully reviewed by a qualified attorney. Preferably, the attorney should have some experience in this specific area of the law since a general release will be ineffective. Strict compliance with the various laws affecting these types of releases is necessary for a valid release.

In fact, the EEOC has said that agreements attempting to require employees to promise not to file EEOC charges or to participate in EEOC investigations may themselves be distinct violations of discrimination laws.[6] So failing to acknowledge an employee's right to file a charge with the EEOC with language such as is provided above may in itself subject the employer to liability for retaliation.

---

[6] EEOC Notice No. 915.002 (April 10, 1997).

Employers should also note that a release cannot protect against future claims or claims that have not yet arisen and that the employee is therefore unaware of. This means that claims for post-employment retaliation cannot be released. Only past or current claims can be released.

▶ Appendix A: Federal Discrimination Laws, Retaliation Provisions

Title VII of the Civil Rights Act of 1964

42 U.S.C. §2000e - 3(a)
Other Unlawful Employment Practices

Sec. 2000e-3. [Section 704]

(a) It shall be an unlawful employment practice for an employer to discriminate against any of his employees or applicants for employment, for an employment agency, or joint labor-management committee controlling apprenticeship or other training or retraining, including on-the-job training programs, to discriminate against any individual, or for a labor organization to discriminate against any member thereof or applicant for membership, because he has opposed any practice made an unlawful employment practice by this subchapter, or because he has made a charge, testified, assisted, or participated in any manner in an investigation, proceeding, or hearing under this subchapter.

(b) It shall be an unlawful employment practice for an employer, labor organization, employment agency, or joint labor-management committee controlling apprenticeship or other training or retraining, including on-the-job training programs, to print or publish or cause to be printed or published any notice or advertisement relating to employment by such an employer or membership in or any classification or referral for employment by such a labor organization, or relating to any classification or referral for employment by such an employment agency, or relating to admission to, or employment in, any program established to provide apprenticeship or other training by such a joint labor-management committee, indicating any preference, limitation, specification, or discrimination, based on race, color, religion, sex, or national origin, except that such a notice or advertisement may indicate a preference, limitation, specification, or discrimination based on religion, sex, or national origin when religion, sex, or national origin is a bona fide occupational qualification for employment.

* * *

The Age Discrimination in Employment Act of 1967

29 U.S.C. §623(d)

Sec. 623. [Section 4]

(d) It shall be unlawful for an employer to discriminate against any of his employees or applicants for employment, for an employment agency to discriminate against any individual, or for a labor organization to discriminate against any member thereof or applicant for membership, because such individual, member or applicant for membership has opposed any practice made unlawful by this section, or because such individual, member or applicant for membership has made a charge, testified, assisted, or participated in any manner in an investigation, proceeding, or litigation under this chapter.

* * *

Americans with Disabilities Act

42 U.S.C. §12203(a) and (b)
Prohibition Against Retaliation and Coercion.

Sec. 12203. [Sec. 503.]

(a) RETALIATION.—No person shall discriminate against any individual because such individual has opposed any act or practice made unlawful by this chapter or because such individual made a charge, testified, assisted, or participated in any manner in an investigation, proceeding, or hearing under this chapter.

(b) INTERFERENCE, COERCION, OR INTIMIDATION.—It shall be unlawful to coerce, intimidate, threaten, or interfere with any individual in the exercise or enjoyment of, or on account of his or her having exercised or enjoyed, or on account of his or her having aided or encouraged any other individual in the exercise or enjoyment of, any right granted or protected by this chapter.

* * *

Fair Labor Standards Act
(Title 29 United States Code, Chapter 8)
§215 Prohibited acts; Prima facie evidence

(a) After the expiration of one hundred and twenty days from the date of enactment of this Act [enacted June 25, 1938], it shall be unlawful for any person—

(3) to discharge or in any other manner discriminate against any employee because such employee has filed any complaint or instituted or caused to be instituted any proceeding under or related to this Act, or has testified or is about to testify in any such proceeding, or has served or is about to serve on an industry committee.

▶ Appendix B: EEOC Guidance

EEOC Directives Transmittal

Number 915.003
Date 5/20/98

SUBJECT: EEOC COMPLIANCE MANUAL

PURPOSE: This transmittal covers the issuance of Section 8 of the new Compliance Manual on "Retaliation". The section provides guidance and instructions for investigating and analyzing claims of retaliation under the statutes enforced by the EEOC.

EFFECTIVE
DATE: Upon receipt

DISTRIBUTION: EEOC Compliance Manual holders

OBSOLETE
DATA: Section 614 of Compliance Manual, Volume 2

FILING
INSTRUCTIONS: This is the first section issued as part of the new Compliance Manual. Section 614 of the existing Compliance Manual should be discarded.

_____ /s/ _____

Paul M. Igasaki
Chairman

Section 8: Retaliation
Table of Contents

Charge-Processing Outline

In processing a charge involving an allegation of retaliation, consider the following issues: There are three essential elements of a retaliation claim:

1) protected activity — opposition to discrimination or participation in the statutory complaint process

2) adverse action

3) causal connection between the protected activity and the adverse action

I. Protected Activity

    A. Did CP oppose discrimination?

        1. Did the charging party (CP) explicitly or implicitly communicate to the respondent (R) or another covered entity a belief that its activity constituted unlawful discrimination under Title VII, the ADA, the ADEA, or the EPA?

            -   If the protest was broad or ambiguous, would CP's protest reasonably have been interpreted as opposition to such unlawful discrimination?

            -   Did someone closely associated with CP oppose discrimination?

        2. Was the manner of opposition reasonable? Was the manner of opposition so disruptive that it significantly interfered with R's legitimate business concerns?

            -   If the manner of opposition was not reasonable, CP is not protected under the anti-retaliation clauses.

        3. Did CP have a reasonable and good faith belief that the opposed practice violated the anti- discrimination laws?

            -   If so, CP is protected against retaliation, even if s/he was mistaken about the unlawfulness of the challenged practices.

            -   If not, CP is not protected under the anti-retaliation clauses.

    B. Did CP participate in the statutory complaint process?

        Did CP or someone closely associated with CP file a charge, or testify, assist, or participate in any manner in an investigation, proceeding, hearing, or lawsuit under the statutes enforced by the EEOC?

        -   If so, CP is protected against retaliation regardless of the validity or reasonableness of the original allegation of discrimination.

        -   CP is protected against retaliation by a respondent for participating in statutory complaint proceedings even if that complaint involved a different covered entity.

II. Adverse Action

    Did R subject CP to any kind of adverse treatment?

    -   Adverse actions undertaken after CP's employment relationship with R ended, such as negative job references, can be challenged.

- Although trivial annoyances are not actionable, more significant retaliatory treatment that is reasonably likely to deter protected activity is unlawful. There is no requirement that the adverse action materially affect the terms, conditions, or privileges of employment.

III. Causal Connection

   A. Is there direct evidence that retaliation was a motive for the adverse action?

      1. Did R official admit that it undertook the adverse action because of the protected activity?

      2. Did R official express bias against CP based on the protected activity? If so, is there evidence linking that statement of bias to the adverse action?

         - Such a link would be established if, for example, the statement was made by the decision-maker at the time of the challenged action.

      If there is direct evidence that retaliation was a motive for the adverse action, "cause" should be found. Evidence as to any additional legitimate motive would be relevant only to relief, under a mixed-motives analysis.

   B. Is there circumstantial evidence that retaliation was the true reason for the adverse action?

      1. Is there evidence raising an inference that retaliation was the cause of the adverse action?

         - Such an inference is raised if the adverse action took place shortly after the protected activity and if the decision-maker was aware of the protected activity before undertaking the adverse action.

         - If there was a long period of time between the protected activity and the adverse action, determine whether there is other evidence raising an inference that the cause of the adverse action was retaliation.

      2. Has R produced evidence of a legitimate, nondiscriminatory reason for the adverse action?

      3. Is R's explanation a pretext designed to hide retaliation?

         - Did R treat similarly situated employees who did not engage in protected activity differently from CP?

         - Did R subject CP to heightened scrutiny after s/he engaged in protected activity?

      If, on the basis of all of the evidence, the investigator is persuaded that retaliation was the true reason for the adverse action, then "cause" should be found.

IV. Special Remedies Issues

   A. Is it appropriate to seek temporary or preliminary relief pending final disposition of the charge?

      1. Is there a substantial likelihood that the challenged action will be found to constitute unlawful retaliation?

      2. Will the retaliation cause irreparable harm to CP and/or the EEOC?

         - Will CP likely incur irreparable harm beyond financial hardship because of the retaliation?

- If the retaliation appears to be based on CP's filing of a prior EEOC charge, will that retaliation likely cause irreparable harm to EEOC's ability to investigate CP's original charge of discrimination?

If there is a substantial likelihood that the challenged action will constitute retaliation and if that retaliation will cause irreparable harm to CP and/or the EEOC, contact the Regional Attorney about pursuing temporary or preliminary relief.

B. Are compensatory and punitive damages available and appropriate?

Compensatory and punitive damages are available for retaliation claims under all of the statutes enforced by the EEOC, including the ADEA and the EPA. Compensatory and punitive damages for retaliation claims under the ADEA and the EPA are not subject to statutory caps.

Punitive damages often are appropriate in retaliation claims under any of the statutes enforced by the EEOC.

Section 614 of EEOC Compliance Manual, Volume 2

8-I INTRODUCTION

A. OVERVIEW

Title VII of the Civil Rights Act of 1964,[1] the Age Discrimination in Employment Act,[2] the Americans with Disabilities Act,[3] and the Equal Pay Act[4] prohibit retaliation by an employer, employment agency, or labor organization because an individual has engaged in protected activity.[5] Protected activity consists of the following:

PROTECTED ACTIVITY

(1) opposing a practice made unlawful by one of the employment discrimination statutes (the "opposition" clause); or

(2) filing a charge, testifying, assisting, or participating in any manner in an investigation, proceeding, or hearing under the applicable statute (the "participation" clause).

This chapter reaffirms the Commission's policy of ensuring that individuals who oppose unlawful employment discrimination, participate in employment discrimination proceedings, or otherwise assert their rights under the laws enforced by the Commission are protected against retaliation. Voluntary compliance with and effective enforcement of the anti-discrimination statutes depend in large part on the initiative of individuals to oppose employment practices that they reasonably believe to be unlawful, and to file charges of discrimination. If retaliation for such activities were permitted to go unremedied, it would have a chilling effect upon the willingness of individuals to speak out against employment discrimination or to participate in the EEOC's administrative process or other employment discrimination proceedings.

The Commission can sue for temporary or preliminary relief before completing its processing of a retaliation charge if the charging party or the Commission will likely suffer irreparable harm because of the retaliation. The investigator should contact the Regional Attorney early in the investigation if it appears that it may be appropriate to seek such relief. See Section 8-III A. for guidance on the standards for seeking temporary or preliminary relief.

---

[1] Section 704(a) of Title VII, 42 U.S.C. § 2000e-3(a).

[2] Section 4(d) of the ADEA, 29 U.S.C. § 623(d).

[3] Section 503(a) of the ADA, 42 U.S.C. § 12203(a). Section 503 (b) of the ADA, 42 U.S.C.12203(b), further provides that it is unlawful "to coerce, intimidate, threaten, or interfere with anyindividual in the exercise or enjoyment of, or on account of his or her having exercised or enjoyed,or on account of his or her having aided or encouraged any other individual in the exercise orenjoyment of, any right granted or protected by this chapter."

[4] Section 15(a)(3) of the Fair Labor Standards Act (FLSA), 29 U.S.C. § 215(a)(3).

[5] Federal employees are also protected against retaliation under each of the employment discrimination statutes. See, *e.g.*, *Hale v. Marsh*, 808 F.2d 616, 619 (7th Cir. 1986) (recognizing retaliation cause of action for federal employees under Title VII); *Bornholdt v. Brady*, 869 F.2d 57, 62 (2d Cir. 1989) (recognizing retaliation cause of action for federal employees under ADEA).

B. BASIS FOR FILING A CHARGE

A charging party who alleges retaliation under Title VII, the ADA, the ADEA, or the EPA need not also allege that he was treated differently because of race, religion, sex, national origin, age, or disability.[6] A charging party who alleges retaliation in violation of the ADA need not be a qualified individual with a disability.[7] Similarly, a charging party who alleges retaliation for protesting discrimination against persons in the protected age group need not be in the protected age group in order to bring an ADEA claim.[8]

A charging party can challenge retaliation by a respondent even if the retaliation occurred after their employment relationship ended.[9] S/he can also challenge retaliation by a respondent based on his/her protected activity involving a different employer, or based on protected activity by someone closely related to or associated with the charging party.[10]

A charging party can bring an ADA retaliation claim against an individual supervisor, as well as an employer. This is because Section 503(a) of the ADA makes it unlawful for a "person" to retaliate against an individual for engaging in protected activity.[11]

8-II. ELEMENTS OF A RETALIATION CLAIM

A. OVERVIEW

There are three essential elements of a retaliation claim:

ELEMENTS OF RETALIATION

1) opposition to discrimination or participation in covered proceedings

2) adverse action

3) causal connection between the protected activity and the adverse action

---

B. PROTECTED ACTIVITY: OPPOSITION

1. Definition

The anti-retaliation provisions make it unlawful to discriminate against an individual because s/he has opposed any practice made unlawful under the employment

---

[6] Where it appears that a charging party's allegation of unlawful retaliation may also be subject to the jurisdiction of another federal agency or a state or local government, s/he should be referred promptly to the appropriate office. For example, if the charging party is covered by a collective bargaining agreement and is a member of the union, s/he should be referred to the NLRB to be counseled on unlawful retaliation under the National Labor Relations Act. Non-payment of overtime pay should be directed to the Department of Labor, Wage and Hour Division. The EEOC office should proceed with its investigation of allegations under its jurisdiction, and refer to any applicable memorandum of understanding or coordination rule with the agency that also has jurisdiction over the matter.

[7] *Krouse v. American Sterilizer*, 126 F.3d 494 (3d Cir. 1997).

[8] *Anderson v. Phillips Petroleum*, 722 F. Supp. 668, 671-72 (D. Kan. 1989).

[9] See Section 8-II D.

[10] See Sections 8-II B.3.c. and d. and 8-II C.3. and 4.

[11] *Ostrach v. Regents of University of California*, 957 F. Supp. 196 (E.D. Calif. 1997) (individual can be sued for retaliation under section 503 of ADA).

discrimination statutes.[12] This protection applies if an individual explicitly or implicitly communicates to his or her employer or other covered entity a belief that its activity constitutes a form of employment discrimination that is covered by any of the statutes enforced by the EEOC.

While Title VII and the ADEA prohibit retaliation based on opposition to a practice made unlawful by those statutes, the ADA prohibits retaliation based on opposition to "any act or practice made unlawful by this chapter." The referenced chapter prohibits not only disability-based employment discrimination, but also disability discrimination in state and local government services, public accommodations, commercial facilities, and telecommunications. Thus, the ADA prohibits retaliation for opposing not just allegedly discriminatory employment practices but also practices made unlawful by the other titles of the statute.

2. Examples of Opposition

* Threatening to file a charge or other formal complaint alleging discrimination

    Threatening to file a complaint with the Commission, a state fair employment practices agency, union, court, or any other entity that receives complaints relating to discrimination is a form of opposition.

    Example - CP tells her manager that if he fails to raise her salary to that of a male coworker who performs the same job, she will file a lawsuit under either the federal Equal Pay Act or under her state's parallel law. This statement constitutes "opposition."

    ---

* Complaining to anyone about alleged discrimination against oneself or others

    A complaint or protest about alleged employment discrimination to a manager, union official, co-worker, company EEO official, attorney, newspaper reporter, Congressperson, or anyone else constitutes opposition. Opposition may be nonverbal, such as picketing or engaging in a production slow-down. Furthermore, a complaint on behalf of another, or by an employee's representative, rather than by the employee herself, constitutes protected opposition by both the person who makes the complaint and the person on behalf of whom the complaint is made.

    A complaint about an employment practice constitutes protected opposition only if the individual explicitly or implicitly communicates a belief that the practice constitutes unlawful employment discrimination.[13] Because individuals often may not know the specific requirements of the anti-discrimination laws enforced by the EEOC, they may make broad or ambiguous complaints of unfair treatment.

---

[12] The anti-retaliation provision of the Fair Labor Standards Act, which applies to the Equal Pay Act, does not contain a specific "opposition" clause. However, courts have recognized that the statute prohibits retaliation based on opposition to allegedly unlawful practices. See, *e.g., EEOC v. Romeo Community Sch.*, 976 F.2d 985, 989-90 (6th Cir. 1992); *EEOC v. White & Son Enterprises*, 881 F.2d 1006, 1011 (11th Cir. 1989). *Contra Lambert v. Genessee Hospital*, 10 F.3d 46, 55 (2d Cir. 1993), *cert. denied*, 511 U.S. 1052 (1994).

[13] See, *e.g., Barber v. CSX Distrib. Services*, 68 F.3d 694 (3d Cir. 1995) (plaintiff's letter to defendant's human resources department complaining about unfair treatment and expressing dissatisfaction that job he sought went to a less qualified individual did not constitute ADEA opposition because letter did not explicitly or implicitly allege that age was reason for alleged unfairness).

Such a protest is protected opposition if the complaint would reasonably have been interpreted as opposition to employment discrimination.

Example 1 - CP calls the President of R's parent company to protest religious discrimination by R. CP's protest constitutes "opposition."

Example 2 - CP complains to co-workers about harassment of a disabled employee by a supervisor. This complaint constitutes "opposition."

Example 3 - CP complains to her foreman about graffiti in her workplace that is derogatory toward women. Although CP does not specify that she believes the graffiti creates a hostile work environment based on sex, her complaint reasonably would have been interpreted by the foreman as opposition to sex discrimination, due to the sex-based content of the graffiti. Her complaint therefore constitutes "opposition."

Example 4 - CP (African-American) requests a wage increase from R, arguing that he deserves to get paid a higher salary. He does not state or suggest a belief that he is being subjected to wage discrimination based on race. There also is no basis to conclude that R would reasonably have interpreted his complaint as opposition to race discrimination because the challenged unfairness could have been based on any of several reasons. CP's protest therefore does not constitute protected "opposition.

---

*   Refusing to obey an order because of a reasonable belief that it is discriminatory

Refusal to obey an order constitutes protected opposition if the individual reasonably believes that the order requires him or her to carry out unlawful employment discrimination.

Example - CP works for an employment agency. His manager instructs him not to refer any African-Americans to a particular client, based on the client's request. CP refuses to obey the order and refers an African-American applicant to that client. CP's action constitutes "opposition."

Refusal to obey an order also constitutes protected opposition if the individual reasonably believes that the order makes discrimination a term or condition of employment. For example, in one case a court recognized that a correction officer's refusal to cooperate with the defendant's practice of allowing white but not black inmates to shower after work shifts constituted protected opposition. Even if the inmates were not "employees," the plaintiff could show that his enforcement of the policy made race discrimination a term or condition of his employment. Thus, his refusal to obey the order constituted opposition to an unlawful employment practice.[14]

---

[14] *Moyo v. Gomez*, 40 F.3d 982 (9th Cir. 1994), *cert. denied*, 513 U.S. 1081 (1995).

* Requesting reasonable accommodation or religious accommodation

A request for reasonable accommodation of a disability constitutes protected activity under Section 503 of the ADA. Although a person making such a request might not literally "oppose" discrimination or "participate" in the administrative or judicial complaint process, s/he is protected against retaliation for making the request. As one court stated,

> It would seem anomalous . . . to think Congress intended no retaliation protection for employees who request a reasonable accommodation unless they also file a formal charge. This would leave employees unprotected if an employer granted the accommodation and shortly thereafter terminated the employee in retaliation.[15]

By the same rationale, persons requesting religious accommodation under Title VII are protected against retaliation for making such requests.

3. Standards Governing Application of the Opposition Clause

Although the opposition clause in each of the EEO statutes is broad, it does not protect every protest against job discrimination. The following principles apply:

a. Manner of Opposition Must Be Reasonable

The manner in which an individual protests perceived employment discrimination must be reasonable in order for the anti-retaliation provisions to apply. In applying a "reasonableness" standard, courts and the Commission balance the right of individuals to oppose employment discrimination and the public's interest in enforcement of the EEO laws against an employer's need for a stable and productive work environment.

Public criticism of alleged discrimination may be a reasonable form of opposition. Courts have protected an employee's right to inform an employer's customers about the employer's alleged discrimination, as well as the right to engage in peaceful picketing to oppose allegedly discriminatory employment practices.[16]

On the other hand, courts have found that the following activities were not reasonable and thus not protected: searching and photocopying confidential documents relating to alleged ADEA discrimination and showing them to co-workers;[17] making an overwhelming number of complaints based on unsupported allegations and bypassing the chain of command in bringing the complaints;[18] and badgering a subordinate employee to give a witness statement in support of an EEOC charge and attempting to coerce her to change her

---

[15] *Soileau v. Guilford of Maine*, 105 F.3d 12, 16 (1st Cir. 1997). See also *Garza v. Abbott Laboratories*, 940 F. Supp. 1227, 1294 (N.D. Ill. 1996) (plaintiff engaged in statutorily protected expression by requesting accommodation for her disability). The courts in *Soileau* and *Garza* only considered whether accommodation requests fall within the opposition or participation clause in Section 503(a) of the ADA. Note, however, that Section 503(b) more broadly makes it unlawful to interfere with "the exercise or enjoyment of . . . any right granted or protected" by the statute.

[16] See, *e.g.*, *Sumner v. United States Postal Service*, 899 F.2d 203 (2d Cir. 1990) (practices protected by opposition clause include writing letters to customers criticizing employer's alleged discrimination).

[17] *O'Day v. McDonnell Douglas Helicopter Co.*, 79 F.3d 756 (9th Cir. 1996).

[18] *Rollins v. Florida Dep't of Law Enforcement*, 868 F.2d 397 (11th Cir. 1989).

statement.[19] Similarly, unlawful activities, such as acts or threats of violence to life or property, are not protected.

If an employee's protests against allegedly discriminatory employment practices interfere with job performance to the extent that they render him or her ineffective in the job, the retaliation provisions do not immunize the worker from appropriate discipline or discharge.[20] Opposition to perceived discrimination does not serve as license for the employee to neglect job duties.

b. Opposition Need Only Be Based on Reasonable and Good Faith Belief

A person is protected against retaliation for opposing perceived discrimination if s/he had a reasonable and good faith belief that the opposed practices were unlawful. Thus, it is well settled that a violation of the retaliation provision can be found whether or not the challenged practice ultimately is found to be unlawful.[21] As one court has stated, requiring a finding of actual illegality would "undermine Title VII's central purpose, the elimination of employment discrimination by informal means; destroy one of the chief means of achieving that purpose, the frank and non-disruptive exchange of ideas between employers and employees; and serve no redeeming statutory or policy purposes of its own."[22]

Example 1 - CP complains to her office manager that her supervisor failed to promote her because of her gender. (She believes that sex discrimination occurred because she was qualified for the promotion and the supervisor promoted a male instead.) CP has engaged in protected opposition regardless of whether the promotion decision was in fact discriminatory because she had a reasonable and good faith belief that discrimination occurred.

Example 2 - Same as above, except the job sought by CP was in accounting and required a CPA license, which CP lacked and the selectee had. CP knew that it was necessary to have a CPA license to perform this job. CP has not engaged in protected opposition because she did not have a reasonable and good faith belief that she was rejected because of sex discrimination.

---

c. Person Claiming Retaliation Need Not Be the Person Who Engaged in Opposition

Title VII, the ADEA, the EPA, and the ADA prohibit retaliation against someone so closely related to or associated with the person exercising his or her statutory rights that it would discourage that person from pursuing those rights.[23] For

---

[19] *Jackson v. St. Joseph State Hospital*, 840 F.2d 1387 (8th Cir.), *cert. denied*, 488 U.S. 892 (1988).

[20] See, *e.g.*, *Coutu v. Martin County Bd. of Comm'rs*, 47 F.3d 1068, 1074 (11th Cir. 1995) (no retaliation found where plaintiff was criticized by her supervisor not because she was opposing discrimination but because she was spending an inordinate amount of time in "employee advocacy" activities and was not completing other aspects of her personnel job).

[21] This standard has been adopted by every circuit that has considered the issue. See, *e.g.*, *Little v. United Technologies*, 103 F.3d 956, 960 (11th Cir. 1997), and *Trent v. Valley Electric Association, Inc.*, 41 F.3d 524, 526 (9th Cir. 1994).

[22] *Berg v. La Crosse Cooler Co.*, 612 F.2d 1041, 1045 (7th Cir. 1980).

[23] See, *e.g.*, *Murphy v. Cadillac Rubber & Plastics, Inc.*, 946 F. Supp. 1108, 1118 (W.D. N.Y. 1996) (plaintiff stated claim of retaliation where he was subjected to adverse action based on his wife's protected activities).

example, it is unlawful to retaliate against an employee because his son, who is also an employee, opposed allegedly unlawful employment practices. Retaliation against a close relative of an individual who opposed discrimination can be challenged by both the individual who engaged in protected activity and the relative, where both are employees. See Section 8-II C.3. for discussion of similar principle under "participation" clause.

d. Practices Opposed Need Not Have Been Engaged in by the Named Respondent

There is no requirement that the entity charged with retaliation be the same as the entity whose allegedly discriminatory practices were opposed by the charging party. For example, a violation would be found if a respondent refused to hire the charging party because it was aware that she opposed her previous employer's allegedly discriminatory practices.

C. PROTECTED ACTIVITY: PARTICIPATION

1. Definition

The anti-retaliation provisions make it unlawful to discriminate against any individual because s/he has made a charge, testified, assisted, or participated in any manner in an investigation, proceeding, hearing, or litigation under Title VII, the ADEA, the EPA, or the ADA. This protection applies to individuals challenging employment discrimination under the statutes enforced by EEOC in EEOC proceedings, in state administrative or court proceedings, as well as in federal court proceedings, and to individuals who testify or otherwise participate in such proceedings.[24] Protection under the participation clause extends to those who file untimely charges. In the federal sector, once a federal employee initiates contact with an EEO counselor, (s)he is engaging in "participation."[25]

2. Participation Is Protected Regardless of Whether the Allegations in the Original Charge Were Valid or Reasonable

The anti-discrimination statutes do not limit or condition in any way the protection against retaliation for participating in the charge process. While the opposition clause applies only to those who protest practices that they reasonably and in good faith believe are unlawful, the participation clause applies to all individuals who participate in the statutory complaint process. Thus, courts have consistently held that a respondent is liable for retaliating against an individual for filing an EEOC charge regardless of the validity or reasonableness of the charge.[26] To permit an employer to retaliate against a charging party based on its unilateral determination that the charge was unreasonable or otherwise unjustified would chill the rights of all individuals protected by the anti-discrimination statutes.

---

[24] The participation clause protects those who testify in an employment discrimination case about their own discriminatory conduct, even if such testimony is involuntary. For example, in *Merritt v. Dillard Paper Co.*, 120 F.3d 1181 (11th Cir. 1997), the defendant fired the plaintiff after he reluctantly testified in his co-worker's Title VII case about workplace sexual activities in which he participated. The president of the defendant company told the plaintiff at the time of his termination that his testimony was "the most damning" to the defendant's case. The court found that this comment constituted direct evidence of retaliation.

[25] *Hashimoto v. Dalton*, 118 F.3d 671, 680 (9th Cir. 1997).

[26] See, *e.g.*, *Wyatt v. Boston*, 35 F.3d 13, 15 (1st Cir. 1994).

3. Person Claiming Retaliation Need Not Be the Person Who Engaged in Participation

The retaliation provisions of Title VII, the ADEA, the EPA, and the ADA prohibit retaliation against someone so closely related to or associated with the person exercising his or her statutory rights that it would discourage or prevent the person from pursuing those rights. For example, it would be unlawful for a respondent to retaliate against an employee because his or her spouse, who is also an employee, filed an EEOC charge.[27] Both spouses, in such circumstances, could bring retaliation claims.

4. The Practices Challenged in Prior or Pending Statutory Proceedings Need Not Have Been Engaged in by the Named Respondent

An individual is protected against retaliation for participation in employment discrimination proceedings even if those proceedings involved a different entity.[28] For example, a violation would be found if a respondent refused to hire the charging party because it was aware that she filed an EEOC charge against her former employer.

D. ADVERSE ACTION

1. General Types of Adverse Actions

The most obvious types of retaliation are denial of promotion, refusal to hire, denial of job benefits, demotion, suspension, and discharge. Other types of adverse actions include threats, reprimands, negative evaluations, harassment, or other adverse treatment.

Suspending or limiting access to an internal grievance procedure also constitutes an "adverse action." For example, in *EEOC v. Board of Governors of State Colleges & Universities*,[29] a university's collective bargaining agreement provided for a specific internal grievance procedure leading to arbitration. The agreement further provided that this procedure could be terminated if the employee sought resolution in any other forum, such as the EEOC. The Seventh Circuit ruled that termination of the grievance process constituted an adverse employment action in violation of the anti-retaliation clause of the ADEA.[30]

2. Adverse Actions Can Occur After the Employment Relationship Between the Charging Party and Respondent Has Ended

In *Robinson v. Shell Oil Company*,[31] the Supreme Court unanimously held that Title VII prohibits respondents from retaliating against former employees as well as current employees for participating in any proceeding under Title VII or opposing any practice made unlawful by that Act. The plaintiff in *Robinson* alleged that his former

---

[27] See, *e.g.*, *EEOC v. Ohio Edison Co.*, 7 F.3d 541, 544 (6th Cir. 1993) (agreeing that plaintiff's allegation of reprisal for relative's protected activities states claim under Title VII); *Thurman v. Robertshaw Control Co.*, 869 F. Supp. 934, 941 (N.D. Ga. 1994) (plaintiff could make out first element of prima facie case of retaliation by showing that plaintiff's close relative participated in the complaint process).

The Commission disagrees with the Fifth Circuit's holding in *Holt v. JTM Indus.*, 89 F.3d 1224 (5th Cir. 1996), *cert. denied*, 117 S.Ct. 1821 (1997), that there was no unlawful retaliation where the plaintiff was put on paid administrative leave because his wife had filed an age discrimination charge.

[28] See, *e.g.*, *Christopher v. Stouder Memorial Hosp.*, 936 F.2d 870, 873-74 (6th Cir.) (defendant's frequent reference to plaintiff's sex discrimination action against prior employer warranted inference that defendant's refusal to hire was retaliatory), *cert. denied*, 502 U.S. 1013 (1991).

[29] 957 F.2d 424 (7th Cir.), *cert. denied*, 506 U.S. 906 (1992).

[30] See also *Johnson v. Palma*, 931 F.2d 203 (2d Cir. 1991) (union's refusal to proceed with plaintiff's grievance after he filed race discrimination complaint with state agency constituted unlawful retaliation).

[31] ___ U.S. ___, 117 S. Ct. 843 (1997).

employer gave him a negative job reference in retaliation for his having filed an EEOC charge against it. Some courts previously had held that former employees could not challenge retaliation that occurred after their employment had ended because Title VII, the ADEA, and the EPA prohibit retaliation against "any employee."[32] However, the Supreme Court stated that coverage of post-employment retaliation is more consistent with the broader context of the statute and with the statutory purpose of maintaining unfettered access to the statute's remedial mechanisms. The Court's holding applies to each of the statutes enforced by the EEOC because of the similar language and common purpose of the anti-retaliation provisions.

Examples of post-employment retaliation include actions that are designed to interfere with the individual's prospects for employment, such as giving an unjustified negative job reference, refusing to provide a job reference, and informing an individual's prospective employer about the individual's protected activity.[33] However, a negative job reference about an individual who engaged in protected activity does not constitute unlawful retaliation unless the reference was based on a retaliatory motive. The truthfulness of the information in the reference may serve as a defense unless there is proof of pretext, such as evidence that the former employer routinely declines to offer information about its former employees' job performance and violated that policy with regard to an individual who engaged in protected activity. See Section 8-II E. below.

Retaliatory acts designed to interfere with an individual's prospects for employment are unlawful regardless of whether they cause a prospective employer to refrain from hiring the individual.[34] As the Third Circuit stated, "an employer who retaliates cannot escape liability merely because the retaliation falls short of its intended result."[35] However, the fact that the reference did not affect the individual's job prospects may affect the relief that is due.

3. Adverse Actions Need Not Qualify as "Ultimate Employment Actions" or Materially Affect the Terms or Conditions of Employment to Constitute Retaliation

Some courts have held that the retaliation provisions apply only to retaliation that takes the form of ultimate employment actions.[36] Others have construed the provisions more broadly, but have required that the action materially affect the terms, conditions, or privileges of employment.[37]

The Commission disagrees with those decisions and concludes that such constructions are unduly restrictive. The statutory retaliation clauses prohibit any adverse treatment that is based on a retaliatory motive and is reasonably likely to deter the charging party or

---

[32] The ADA, unlike the other anti-discrimination statutes, prohibits retaliation against "any individual" who has opposed discrimination based on disability or participated in the charge process. 42 U.S.C. § 12203. 33 See, *e.g.*, *EEOC v. L. B. Foster*, 123 F.3d 746 (3d Cir. 1997), *cert. denied*, 66 U.S. L.W. 3388 (U.S. March 2, 1998); *Ruedlinger v. Jarrett*, 106 F.3d 212 (7th Cir. 1997).

[34] *Hashimoto v. Dalton*, 118 F.3d 671, 676 (9th Cir. 1997).

[35] *EEOC v. L. B. Foster*, 123 F.3d at 754.

[36] See *Ledergerber v. Stangler*, 122 F.3d 1142 (8th Cir. 1997) (reassignment of plaintiff's staff, with attendant loss of status, did not rise to level of ultimate employment decision to constitute actionable retaliation); *Mattern v. Eastman Kodak Co.*, 104 F.3d 702 (5th Cir.) (anti-retaliation provisions only bar "ultimate employment actions" that are retaliatory; harassment, reprimands, and poor evaluation could not be challenged), *cert. denied*, 118 S. Ct. 336 (1997).

[37] See, *e.g.*, *Munday v. Waste Management of North America*, 126 F.3d 239 (4th Cir. 1997) (employer's instruction to workers to shun plaintiff who had engaged in protected activity, to spy on her, and to report back to management whatever she said to them did not adversely affect plaintiff's terms, condition, or benefits of employment and therefore could not be challenged), *cert. denied*, 118 S. Ct. 1053 (1998).

---

others from engaging in protected activity. Of course, petty slights and trivial annoyances are not actionable, as they are not likely to deter protected activity. More significant retaliatory treatment, however, can be challenged regardless of the level of harm. As the Ninth Circuit has stated, the degree of harm suffered by the individual "goes to the issue of damages, not liability."[38]

Example 1 - CP filed a charge alleging that he was racially harassed by his supervisor and co-workers. After learning about the charge, CP's manager asked two employees to keep CP under surveillance and report back about his activities. The surveillance constitutes an "adverse action" that is likely to deter protected activity, and is unlawful if it was conducted because of CP's protected activity.

Example 2 - CP filed a charge alleging that she was denied a promotion because of her gender. One week later, her upervisor invited a few employees out to lunch. CP believed hat the reason he excluded her was because of her EEOC charge. Even if the supervisor chose not to invite CP because of her charge, this would not constitute unlawful retaliation because it is not reasonably likely to deter protected activity.

Example 3 - Same as Example 2, except that CP's supervisor invites all employees in CP's unit to regular weekly lunches. The supervisor excluded CP from these lunches after she filed the sex discrimination charge. If CP was excluded because of her charge, this would constitute unlawful retaliation since it could reasonably deter CP or others from engaging in protected activity.

The Commission's position is based on statutory language and policy considerations. The anti-retaliation provisions are exceptionally broad. They make it unlawful "to discriminate" against an individual because of his or her protected activity. This is in contrast to the general anti-discrimination provisions which make it unlawful to discriminate with respect to an individual's "terms, conditions, or privileges of employment." The retaliation provisions set no qualifiers on the term "to discriminate," and therefore prohibit any discrimination that is reasonably likely to deter protected activity.[39] They do not restrict the actions that can be challenged to those that affect the terms and conditions of employment.[40] Thus, a violation will be found

---

[38] *Hashimoto*, 118 F.3d at 676. See also *EEOC v. L. B. Foster*, 123 F.3d at 754 n.4 (plaintiff need not prove that retaliatory denial of job reference caused prospective employer to reject her; such a showing is relevant only to damages, not liability); *Smith v. Secretary of Navy*, 659 F.2d 1113, 1120 (D.C. Cir. 1981) ("the questions of statutory violation and appropriate statutory remedy are conceptually distinct. An illegal act of discrimination — whether based on race or some other factor such as a motive of reprisal — is a wrong in itself under Title VII, regardless of whether that wrong would warrant an award of [damages]").

[39] See, *e.g.*, *Knox v. State of Indiana*, 93 F.3d 1327, 1334 (7th Cir. 1996) ("[t]here is nothing in the law of retaliation that restricts the type of retaliatory act that might be visited upon an employee who seeks to invoke her rights by filing a complaint"); *Passer v. American Chemical Society*, 935 F.2d 322, 331 (D.C. Cir. 1991) (Section 704(a) broadly prohibits an employer from discriminating against its employees in any way for engaging in protected activity and does not "limit its reach only to acts of retaliation that take the form of cognizable employment actions such as discharge, transfer or demotion").

[40] Even if there were a requirement that the challenged action affect the terms or conditions of employment, retaliatory acts that create a hostile work environment would meet that standard since, as the Supreme Court has made clear, the terms and condition of employment include the intangible work environment. *Meritor Savings Bank v. Vinson*, 477 U.S. 57, 64-67 (1986). For examples of cases recognizing that retaliatory harassment is unlawful, see *DeAngelis v. El Paso Municipal Police Officers Ass'n.*, 51 F.3d 591 (5th Cir.), *cert. denied*, 116 S. Ct. 473 (1995); *Davis v. Tri-State Mack Distributor*, 981 F.2d 340 (8th Cir. 1992).

if an employer retaliates against a worker for engaging in protected activity through threats,[41] harassment in or out of the workplace, or any other adverse treatment that is reasonably likely to deter protected activity by that individual or other employees.[42]

This broad view of coverage accords with the primary purpose of the anti-retaliation provisions, which is to "[m]aintain unfettered access to statutory remedial mechanisms."[43] Regardless of the degree or quality of harm to the particular complainant, retaliation harms the public interest by deterring others from filing a charge.[44] An interpretation of Title VII that permits some forms of retaliation to go unpunished would undermine the effectiveness of the EEO statutes and conflict with the language and purpose of the anti-retaliation provisions.

E. PROOF OF CAUSAL CONNECTION

In order to establish unlawful retaliation, there must be proof that the respondent took an adverse action because the charging party engaged in protected activity. Proof of this retaliatory motive can be through direct or circumstantial evidence. The evidentiary framework that applies to other types of discrimination claims also applies to retaliation claims.

1. Direct Evidence

If there is credible direct evidence that retaliation was a motive for the challenged action, "cause" should be found. Evidence as to any legitimate motive for the challenged action would be relevant only to relief, not to liability.[45]

Direct evidence of a retaliatory motive is any written or verbal statement by a respondent official that s/he undertook the challenged action because the charging party engaged in protected activity. Such evidence also includes a written or oral statement by a

---

[41] See *McKnight v. General Motors Corp.*, 908 F.2d 104, 111 (7th Cir. 1990) ("[r]etaliation or a threat of retaliation is a common method of deterrence"), *cert. denied*, 499 U.S. 919 (1991); *Garcia v. Lawn*, 805 F.2d 1400, 1401-02 (9th Cir. 1986) (threatened transfer to undesirable location); *Atkinson v. Oliver T. Carr Co.*, 40 FEP Cases (BNA) 1041, 1043-44 (D.D.C. 1986) (threat to press criminal complaint).

[42] For examples of cases finding unlawful retaliation based on adverse actions that did not affect the terms or conditions of employment, see *Hashimoto*, 118 F.3d at 675-76 (retaliatory job reference violated Title VII even though it did not cause failure to hire); *Berry v. Stevinson Chevrolet*, 74 F.3d 980, 986 (10th Cir. 1996) (instigating criminal theft and forgery charges against former employee who filed EEOC charge found retaliatory); *Passer*, 935 F.2d at 331 (canceling symposium in honor of retired employee who filed ADEA charge found retaliatory).

[43] *Robinson v. Shell Oil Co.*, 117 S. Ct. 843, 848 (1997).

[44] *Garcia*, 805 F.2d at 1405.

[45] The basis for finding "cause" whenever there is credible direct evidence of a retaliatory motive is Section 107 of the 1991 Civil Rights Act, 42 U.S.C. §§ 2000e-2(m) and 2000e-5(g)(2)(B). Section 107 provides that an unlawful employment practice is established whenever race, color, religion, sex, or national origin was a motivating factor, even though other factors also motivated the practice. It further provides that a complainant who makes such a showing can obtain declaratory relief, injunctive relief, and attorneys fees but no damages or reinstatement if the respondent proves that it would have taken the same action even absent the discrimination. Section 107 partially overrules *Price Waterhouse v. Hopkins*, 490 U.S. 228 (1989), which held that a respondent can avoid liability for intentional discrimination in mixed-motives cases if it can prove that it would have made the same decision in the absence of the discrimination.

Some courts have ruled that Section 107 does not apply to retaliation claims. See, *e.g.*, *Woodson v. Scott Paper*, 109 F.3d 913 (3d Cir.), *cert. denied*, 118 S. Ct. 299 (1997). Those courts apply *Price Waterhouse v. Hopkins*, and therefore absolve the employer of liability for proven retaliation if the establishes that it would have made the same decision in the absence of retaliation. Other courts have applied Section 107 to retaliation claims. See, *e.g.*, *Merritt v. Dillard Paper Co.*, 120 F.3d 1181, 1191 (11th Cir. 1997).

The Commission concludes that Section 107 applies to retaliation. Courts have long held that the evidentiary framework for proving employment discrimination based on race, sex, or other protected class status also applies to claims of discrimination based on retaliation. Furthermore, an interpretation of Section 107 that permits proven retaliation to go unpunished undermines the purpose of the anti-retaliation provisions of maintaining unfettered access to the statutory remedial mechanism.

respondent official that on its face demonstrates a bias toward the charging party based on his or her protected activity, along with evidence linking that bias to the adverse action. Such a link could be shown if the statement was made by the decision-maker at the time of the adverse action.[46] Direct evidence of retaliation is rare.

Example - CP filed a charge against Respondent A, alleging that her supervisor sexually harassed and constructively discharged her. CP subsequently sued A and reached a settlement. When CP applied for a new job with Respondent B, she received a conditional offer subject to a reference check. When B called CP's former supervisor at A Co. for a reference, the supervisor said that CP was a "troublemaker," started a sex harassment lawsuit, and was not anyone B "would want to get mixed up with." B did not hire CP. She suspected that her former supervisor gave her a negative reference and filed retaliation charges against A and B. The EEOC investigator discovered notes memorializing the phone conversation between A and B. These notes are direct evidence of retaliation by A because they prove on their face that A told B about CP's protected activity and that A gave CP a negative reference because of that protected activity. These notes are not direct evidence of retaliation by B because they do not directly prove that B rejected CP because of her protected activity. However, the fact that B gave CP a conditional job offer and then decided not to hire her after learning about her protected activity is strong circumstantial evidence of B's retaliation. (See Section 8-II E.2. below.)

---

2. Circumstantial Evidence

The most common method of proving that retaliation was the reason for an adverse action is through circumstantial evidence. A violation is established if there is circumstantial evidence raising an inference of retaliation and if the respondent fails to produce evidence of a legitimate, non-retaliatory reason for the challenged action, or if the reason advanced by the respondent is a pretext to hide the retaliatory motive.

CIRCUMSTANTIAL EVIDENCE OF RETALIATION

1. Evidence raises inference that retaliation was the cause of the challenged action;

2. Respondent produces evidence of a legitimate, non-retaliatory reason for the challenged action; and

3. Complainant proves that the reason advanced by the respondent is a pretext to hide the retaliatory motive.

---

[46] For example, in *Merritt v. Dillard Paper Company*, 120 F.3d 1181 (11th Cir. 1997), the plaintiff testified in a co-worker's Title VII action about sexual harassment in the workplace. Shortly after the case was settled, the president of the company fired the plaintiff. The court found direct evidence of retaliation based on the president's statement to the plaintiff, "[y]our deposition was the most damning to Dillard's case, and you no longer have a place here at Dillard Paper Company."

An initial inference of retaliation arises where there is proof that the protected activity and the adverse action were related.[47] Typically, the link is demonstrated by evidence that: (1) the adverse action occurred shortly after the protected activity, and (2) the person who undertook the adverse action was aware of the complainant's protected activity before taking the action.

An inference of retaliation may arise even if the time period between the protected activity and the adverse action was long, if there is other evidence that raises an inference of retaliation. For example, in *Shirley v. Chrysler First, Inc.*,[48] a 14-month interval between the plaintiff's filing of an EEOC charge and her termination did not conclusively disprove retaliation where the plaintiff's manager mentioned the EEOC charge at least twice a week during the interim and termination occurred just two months after the EEOC dismissed her charge.[49]

Common non-retaliatory reasons offered by respondents for challenged actions include: poor job performance; inadequate qualifications for the position sought; violation of work rules or insubordination; and, with regard to negative job references, truthfulness of the information in the reference. For example, in one case, the plaintiff claimed that she was discharged for retaliatory reasons but the employer produced unrebutted evidence that she was discharged because of her excessive absenteeism.[50] In another case, the plaintiff alleged that his former employer's negative job reference was retaliatory, but the defendant established that the evaluation was based on the former supervisor's personal observation of the plaintiff during his employment and contemporary business records documenting those observations.[51]

Even if the respondent produces evidence of a legitimate, nondiscriminatory reason for the challenged action, a violation will still be found if this explanation is a pretext designed to hide the true retaliatory motive. Typically, pretext is proved through evidence that the respondent treated the complainant differently from similarly situated employees or that the respondent's explanation for the adverse action is not believable. Pretext can also be shown if the respondent subjected the charging party's work performance to heightened scrutiny after she engaged in protected activity.[52]

Example 1- CP alleges that R denied her a promotion because she opposed the under-representation of women in management jobs and was therefore viewed as a "troublemaker." The promotion went to another female employee. R asserts that the selectee was better qualified for the job because she had a Masters in Business Administration, while CP only had a college degree. The EEOC investigator finds

---

[47] *Simmons v. Camden County Bd. of Educ.*, 757 F.2d 1187, 1189 (11th Cir.), *cert. denied*, 474 U.S. 981 (1985).

[48] 970 F.2d 39 (5th Cir. 1992).

[49] See *Kachmar v. Sunguard Data Systems*, 109 F.3d 173 (3d Cir. 1997) (district court erroneously dismissed plaintiff's retaliation claim because termination occurred nearly one year after her protected activity; when there may be reasons why adverse action was not taken immediately, absence of immediacy does not disprove causation).

[50] *Miller v. Vesta, Inc.*, 946 F. Supp. 697 (E.D. Wis. 1996).

[51] *Fields v. Phillips School of Business & Tech.*, 870 F. Supp. 149 (W.D. Tex.), *aff'd mem.*, 59 F.3d 1242 (5th Cir. 1994).

[52] See, *e.g.*, *Hossaini v. Western Missouri Medical Center*, 97 F.3d 1085 (8th Cir. 1996) (reasonable person could infer that defendant's explanation for plaintiff's discharge was pretextual where defendant launched investigation into allegedly improper conduct by plaintiff shortly after she engaged in protected activity).

that this explanation is pretextual because CP has significantly greater experience working at R Company and experience has always been the most important criterion for selection for management jobs.

Example 2 - CP alleges that R gave him a negative job reference because he had filed an EEOC charge. R produces evidence that its negative statements to CP's prospective employer were honest assessments of CP's job performance. There is no proof of pretext, and therefore the investigator finds no retaliation.

Example 3 - Same as Example 2, except there is evidence that R routinely declines to offer information about former employees' job performance. R fails to offer a credible explanation for why it violated this policy with regard to CP. Therefore, pretext is found.

8-III   SPECIAL REMEDIES ISSUES

A. TEMPORARY OR PRELIMINARY RELIEF

Section 706(f)(2) of Title VII authorizes the Commission to seek temporary injunctive relief before final disposition of a charge when a preliminary investigation indicates that prompt judicial action is necessary to carry out the purposes of Title VII. Section 107 of the ADA incorporates this provision. The ADEA and the EPA do not authorize a court to give interim relief pending resolution of an EEOC charge. However, the EEOC can seek such relief as part of a lawsuit for permanent relief, pursuant to Rule 65 of the Federal Rules of Civil Procedure.

Temporary or preliminary relief allows a court to stop retaliation before it occurs or continues. Such relief is appropriate if there is a substantial likelihood that the challenged action will be found to constitute unlawful retaliation, and if the charging party and/or the EEOC will likely suffer irreparable harm because of the retaliation. Although courts have ruled that financial hardships are not irreparable, other harms that accompany loss of a job may be irreparable. For example, in one case forced retirees showed irreparable harm and qualified for a preliminary injunction where they lost work and future prospects for work, consequently suffering emotional distress, depression, a contracted social life, and other related harms.[53] A temporary injunction also is appropriate if the respondent's retaliation will likely cause irreparable harm to the Commission's ability to investigate the charging party's original charge of discrimination. For example, the retaliation may discourage others from providing testimony or from filing additional charges based on the same or other alleged unlawful acts.[54]

The intake officer or investigator should notify the Regional Attorney when a charge of retaliation is filed and where temporary or preliminary relief may be appropriate.[55]

---

[53] *EEOC v. Chrysler Corp.*, 733 F.2d 1183, 1186 (6th Cir.), *reh'g denied*, 738 F.2d 167 (1984). See also *EEOC v. City of Bowling Green*, Kentucky, 607 F. Supp. 524 (D. Ky. 1985) (granting preliminary injunction preventing defendant from mandatorily retiring policy department employee because of his age; although plaintiff could have collected back pay and been reinstated at later time, he would have suffered from inability to keep up with current matters in police department and would have suffered anxiety or emotional problems due to compulsory retirement).

[54] See, *e.g.*, *Garcia v. Lawn*, 805 F.2d 1400, 1405-06 (9th Cir. 1986) (chilling effect of retaliation on other employee's willingness to exercise their rights or testify for plaintiff constitutes irreparable harm).

[55] 29 C.F.R. § 1601.23 sets forth procedures for seeking preliminary or temporary relief. Section 13.1 of Volume I of the EEOC Compliance Manual sets forth procedures for selecting, developing, and obtaining approval of such cases.

B. COMPENSATORY AND PUNITIVE DAMAGES

1. Availability of Damages for Retaliation Under ADEA and EPA

    A 1977 amendment to the Fair Labor Standards Act authorizes both legal and equitable relief for retaliation claims under that Act.[56] Compensatory and punitive damages therefore are available for retaliation claims brought under the EPA and the ADEA, as well as under Title VII and the ADA.[57] The compensatory and punitive damages obtained under the EPA and the ADEA are not subject to statutory caps.

2. Appropriateness of Punitive Damages

    Proven retaliation frequently constitutes a practice undertaken "with malice or with reckless indifference to the federally protected rights of an aggrieved individual." Therefore, punitive damages often will be appropriate in retaliation claims brought under any of the statutes enforced by the EEOC.[58]

---

[56] 29 U.S.C. § 216(b).

[57] See *Moskowitz v. Trustees of Purdue University*, 5 F.3d 279 (7th Cir. 1993) (FLSA amendment allows common law damages in addition to back wages and liquidated damages where plaintiff is retaliated against for exercising his rights under the ADEA); *Soto v. Adams Elevator Equip. Co.*, 941 F.2d 543 (7th Cir. 1991) (FLSA amendment authorizes compensatory and punitive damages for retaliation claims under the EPA, in addition to lost wages and liquidated damages).

[58] See *Kim v. Nash Finch Co.*, 123 F.3d 1046 (8th Cir. 1997) (evidence of retaliation supported jury finding of reckless indifference to plaintiff's rights; although $7 million award for punitive damages was excessive, district court's lowered award of $300,000 was not).

▶ **Appendix C: U.S. Supreme Court Decision**

CHARLES T. ROBINSON, SR. v. SHELL OIL COMPANY

No. 95-1376
SUPREME COURT OF THE UNITED STATES
Argued November 6, 1996 —— Decided February 18, 1997

Syllabus

After he was fired by respondent, petitioner filed an employment discrimination charge with the Equal Employment Opportunity Commission (EEOC) under Title VII of the Civil Rights Act of 1964. While that charge was pending, petitioner applied for a job with another company, which contacted respondent for an employment reference. Claiming that respondent gave him a negative reference in retaliation for his having filed the EEOC charge, petitioner filed suit under §704(a) of Title VII, which makes it unlawful "for an employer to discriminate against any of his employees or applicants for employment" who have availed themselves of Title VII's protections. The District Court dismissed the action, and the en banc Fourth Circuit affirmed, holding that the term "employees" in §704(a) refers only to current employees and therefore petitioner's claim was not cognizable under Title VII.

Held:: Because the term "employees," as used in §704(a) of Title VII, includes former employees, petitioner may sue respondent for its allegedly retaliatory postemployment actions.

(a) Consideration of the statutory language, the specific context in which it is used, and the broader context of Title VII as a whole leads to the conclusion that the term "employees" in §704(a) is ambiguous as to whether it excludes former employees. First, there is no temporal qualifier in §704(a) such as would make plain that it protects only persons still employed at the time of the retaliation. Second, §701(f)'s general definition of "employee" likewise lacks any temporal qualifier and is consistent with either current or past employment. Third, a number of other Title VII provisions, including §§706(g)(1), 717(b), and 717(c), use the term "employees" to mean something more inclusive or different from

"current employees." That still other sections use the term to refer unambiguously to a current employee, see, *e.g.,* §§703(h), 717(b), at most demonstrates that the term may have a plain meaning in the context of a particular section—not that it has the same meaning in all other sections and in all other contexts. Once it is established that "employees" includes former employees in some sections, but not in others, the term standing alone is necessarily ambiguous and each section must be analyzed to determine whether the context gives the term a definite meaning.

(b) A holding that former employees are included within §704(a)'s coverage is more consistent with the broader context provided by other Title VII sections and with §704(a)'s primary purpose of maintaining unfettered access to Title VII's remedial mechanisms. As noted, several sections of the statute plainly contemplate that former employees will make use of Title VII's remedial mechanisms. These include §703(a), which prohibits discriminatory "discharge." Insofar as §704(a) expressly protects employees from retaliation for filing a "charge," and a charge under §703(a) alleging unlawful discharge would necessarily be brought by a former employee, it is far more consistent to include former employees within the scope of "employees" protected by §704(a). This interpretation is supported by the arguments of petitioner and the EEOC that exclusion of former employees from §704(a) would undermine Title VII's effectiveness by allowing the threat of post-employment retaliation to deter victims of discrimination from complaining to the EEOC, and would provide a perverse incentive for employers to fire employees who might bring Title VII claims.

THOMAS, J., delivered the opinion for a unanimous Court.

Opinion of the Court

JUSTICE THOMAS delivered the opinion of the Court.

Section 704(a) of Title VII of the Civil Rights Act of 1964 makes it unlawful "for an employer to discriminate against any of his employees or applicants for employment" who have either availed themselves of Title VII's protections or assisted others in so doing. 78 Stat. 257, as amended, 42 U.S.C. §2000e-3(a). We are asked to decide in this case whether the term "employees," as used in §704(a), includes former employees, such that petitioner may bring suit against his former employer for postemployment actions allegedly taken in retaliation for petitioner's having filed a charge with the Equal Employment Opportunity Commission (EEOC). The United States Court of Appeals for the Fourth Circuit, sitting en banc, held that the term "employees" in §704(a) referred only to current employees and therefore petitioner's claim was not cognizable under Title VII. We granted certiorari, 517 U.S. 1154 (1996), and now reverse.

I

Respondent Shell Oil Co. fired petitioner Charles T. Robinson, Sr., in 1991. Shortly thereafter, petitioner filed a charge with the EEOC, alleging that respondent had discharged him because of his race. While that charge was pending, petitioner applied for a job with another company. That company contacted respondent, as petitioner's former employer, for an employment reference. Petitioner claims that respondent gave him a negative reference in retaliation for his having filed the EEOC charge.

Petitioner subsequently sued under §704(a), alleging retaliatory discrimination. On respondent's motion, the District Court dismissed the action, adhering to previous Fourth Circuit precedent holding that §704(a) does not apply to former employees. Petitioner appealed, and a divided panel of the Fourth Circuit reversed the District Court. The Fourth Circuit granted rehearing en banc, vacated the panel decision, and thereafter affirmed the District

Court's determination that former employees may not bring suit under §704(a) for retaliation occurring after termination of their employment. 70 F.3d 325 (1995) (en banc).

We granted certiorari in order to resolve a conflict among the Circuits on this issue.[1]

II

A

Our first step in interpreting a statute is to determine whether the language at issue has a plain and unambiguous meaning with regard to the particular dispute in the case. Our inquiry must cease if the statutory language is unambiguous and "the statutory scheme is coherent and consistent." *United States v. Ron Pair Enterprises, Inc.*, 489 U.S. 235, 240, 103 L. Ed. 2d 290, 109 S. Ct. 1026 (1989); see also *Connecticut Nat. Bank v. Germain*, 503 U.S. 249, 253-254, 117 L. Ed. 2d 391, 112 S. Ct. 1146 (1992).

The plainness or ambiguity of statutory language is determined by reference to the language itself, the specific context in which that language is used, and the broader context of the statute as a whole. *Estate of Cowart v. Nicklos Drilling Co.*, 505 U.S. 469, 477, 120 L. Ed. 2d 379, 112 S. Ct. 2589 (1992); *McCarthy v. Bronson*, 500 U.S. 136, 139, 114 L. Ed. 2d 194, 111 S. Ct. 1737 (1991). In this case, consideration of those factors leads us to conclude that the term "employees," as used in §704(a), is

---

[1] The other Courts of Appeals to have considered this issue have held that the term "employees" in §704(a) does include former employees. See *Charlton v. Paramus Bd. of Educ.*, 25 F.3d 194, 198-200 (CA3), *cert. denied*, 513 U.S. 1022, 130 L. Ed. 2d 503, 115 S. Ct. 590 (1994); *Bailey v. USX Corp.*, 850 F.2d 1506, 1509 (CA11 1988); *O'Brien v. Sky Chefs, Inc.*, 670 F.2d 864, 869 (CA9 1982), overruled on other grounds by *Atonio v. Wards Cove Packing Co.*, 810 F.2d 1477, 1481-1482 (CA9 1987) (en banc); *Pantchenko v. C. B. Dolge Co.*, 581 F.2d 1052, 1055 (CA2 1978); *Rutherford v. American Bank of Commerce*, 565 F.2d 1162, 1165 (CA10 1977). The Fourth Circuit indicated that it joined the approach taken by the Seventh Circuit in *Reed v. Shepard*, 939 F.2d 484, 492-493 (1991). But the Seventh Circuit has since repudiated the Fourth Circuit's view of *Reed*. See *Veprinsky v. Fluor Daniel, Inc.*, 87 F.3d 881, 886 (CA7 1996).

ambiguous as to whether it excludes former employees.

At first blush, the term "employees" in §704(a) would seem to refer to those having an existing employment relationship with the employer in question. *Cf. Walters v. Metropolitan Ed. Enterprises, Inc.*, ante, at 207-208 (interpreting the term "employees" in §701(b), 42 U.S.C. §2000e(b)). This initial impression, however, does not withstand scrutiny in the context of §704(a). First, there is no temporal qualifier in the statute such as would make plain that §704(a) protects only persons still employed at the time of the retaliation. That the statute could have expressly included the phrase "former employees" does not aid our inquiry. Congress also could have used the phrase "current employees." But nowhere in Title VII is either phrase used — even where the specific context otherwise makes clear an intent to cover current or former employees.[2] Similarly, that other statutes have been more specific in their coverage of "employees" and "former employees," see, *e.g.,* 2 U.S.C. §301(4) (1994 ed., Supp. I) (defining "employee" to include "former employee"); 5 U.S.C. §1212(a)(1) (including "employees, former employees, and applicants for employment" in the operative provision), proves only that Congress can use the unqualified term "employees" to refer only to current employees, not that it did so in this particular statute.

Second, Title VII's definition of "employee" likewise lacks any temporal qualifier

and is consistent with either current or past employment. Section 701(f) defines "employee" for purposes of Title VII as "an individual employed by an employer." 42 U.S.C. §2000e(f). The argument that the term "employed," as used in §701(f), is commonly used to mean "performing work under an employer-employee relationship," Black's Law Dictionary 525 (6th ed. 1990), begs the question by implicitly reading the word "employed" to mean "is employed." But the word "employed" is not so limited in its possible meanings, and could just as easily be read to mean "was employed."

Third, a number of other provisions in Title VII use the term "employees" to mean something more inclusive or different from "current employees." For example, §§706(g)(1) and 717(b) both authorize affirmative remedial action (by a court or EEOC, respectively) "which may include . . . reinstatement or hiring of employees." 42 U.S.C. §§2000e-5(g)(1) and 2000e-16(b). As petitioner notes, because one does not "reinstate" current employees, that language necessarily refers to former employees. Likewise, one may hire individuals to be employees, but one does not typically hire persons who already are employees.

Section 717(b) requires federal departments and agencies to have equal employment opportunity policies and rules, "which shall include a provision that an employee or applicant for employment shall be notified of any final action taken on any complaint of discrimination filed by him thereunder." 42 U.S.C. §2000e-16(b). If the complaint involves discriminatory discharge, as it often does, the "employee" who must be notified is necessarily a former employee. Similarly, §717(c) provides that an "employee or applicant for employment, if aggrieved by the final disposition of his complaint, . . . may file a civil action . . . ." 42 U.S.C. §2000e-16(c). Again, given that discriminatory discharge is a forbidden" personnel action affecting employees," see §717(a), 42 U.S.C. §2000e-16(a), the term "employee" in §717(c) necessarily includes a former employee. See *Loeffler v. Frank*, 486 U.S. 549, 100 L. Ed. 2d 549, 108 S. Ct. 1965 (1988) (involving a discriminatory discharge action

[2] Our recent decision in *Walters v. Metropolitan Ed. Enterprises, Inc.*, ante, p. 202, held that the term "employees" in §701(b), 42 U.S.C. §2000e(b), referred to those persons with whom an employer has an existing employment relationship. See *ante*, at 207-208. But §701(b) has two significant temporal qualifiers. The provision, which delimits Title VII's coverage, states that the Act applies to any employer "who has fifteen or more employees for each working day in each of twenty or more calendar weeks in the current or preceding calendar year." 42 U.S.C. §2000e(b) (emphasis added). The emphasized words specify the time-frame in which the employment relationship must exist, and thus the specific context of that section did not present the particular ambiguity at issue in the present case.

successfully brought under §717 by a former Postal Service employee).[3]

Of course, there are sections of Title VII where, in context, use of the term "employee" refers unambiguously to a current employee, for example, those sections addressing salary or promotions. See §703(h), 42 U.S.C. §2000e-2(h) (allowing different standards of compensation for "employees who work in different locations"); §717(b), 42 U.S.C. §2000e-16(b) (directing federal agencies to establish a plan "to provide a maximum opportunity for employees to advance so as to perform at their highest potential").

But those examples at most demonstrate that the term "employees" may have a plain meaning in the context of a particular section— not that the term has the same meaning in all other sections and in all other contexts. Once it is established that the term "employees" includes former employees in some sections, but not in others, the term standing alone is necessarily ambiguous and each section must be analyzed to determine whether the context gives the term a further meaning that would resolve the issue in dispute.[4]

Respondent argues that the addition of the word "his" before "employees" narrows the scope of the provision. Brief for Respondent 19. That argument is true, so far as it goes, but it does not resolve the question before us—namely, in what timeframe must the employment relationship exist. The phrase "his employees" could include "his" former employees, but still exclude persons who have never worked for the particular employer being charged with retaliation.

Nor are we convinced by respondent's argument that Congress' inclusion in §704(a) of "applicants for employment" as persons distinct from "employees," coupled with its failure to include "former employees," is evidence of congressional intent not to include former employees. The use of the term "applicants" in §704(a) does not serve to confine, by negative inference, the temporal scope of the term "employees." Respondent's argument rests on the incorrect premise that the term "applicants" is equivalent to the phrase "future employees." But the term "applicants" would seem to cover many persons who will not become employees. Unsuccessful applicants or those who turn down a job offer, for example, would have been applicants, but not future employees. And the term fails to cover certain future employees who may be offered and will accept jobs without having to apply for those jobs. Because the term "applicants" in §704(a) is not synonymous with the phrase "future employees," there is no basis for engaging in the further (and questionable) negative inference that inclusion of the term "applicants" demonstrates intentional exclusion of former employees.

Finally, the use of the term "individual" in §704(a), as well as in §703(a), 42 U.S.C. §2000e-2(a), provides no meaningful assistance in resolving this case. To be sure, "individual" is a broader term than "employee" and would facially seem to cover a former employee. But it would also encompass a present employee as well as other persons who have never had an employment relationship with the employer at issue. The term "individual," therefore, does not seem designed to capture former employees, as distinct from current employees, and its use provides no insight into whether the term "employees" is limited only to current employees.

---

[3] Other sections also seem to use the term "employees" to mean something other than current employees. Section 701(c) defines "employment agency" as "any person regularly undertaking . . . to procure employees for an employer or to procure for employees opportunities to work for an employer . . . ." 42 U.S.C. §2000e(c). This language most naturally is read to mean "prospective employees." Section 701(e) uses identical language when providing that a labor organization affects commerce if it "operates a hiring hall or hiring office which procures employees for an employer . . . ." 42 U.S.C. §2000e(e).

[4] Petitioner's examples of non-Title VII cases using the term "employee" to refer to a former employee are largely irrelevant, except to the extent they tend to rebut a claim that the term "employee" has some intrinsically plain meaning. See, e.g., Richardson v. Belcher, 404 U.S. 78, 81, 83, 30 L. Ed. 2d 231, 92 S. Ct. 254 (1971) (unemployed disabled worker); Nash v. Florida Industrial Comm'n, 389 U.S. 235, 239, 19 L. Ed. 2d 438, 88 S. Ct. 362 (1967) (individual who had been fired); Flemming v. Nestor, 363 U.S. 603, 611, 4 L. Ed. 2d 1435, 80 S. Ct. 1367 (1960) (retired worker).

B

Finding that the term "employees" in §704(a) is ambiguous, we are left to resolve that ambiguity. The broader context provided by other sections of the statute provides considerable assistance in this regard. As noted above, several sections of the statute plainly contemplate that former employees will make use of the remedial mechanisms of Title VII. See *supra*, 519 U.S. at 342-343. Indeed, §703(a) expressly includes discriminatory "discharge" as one of the unlawful employment practices against which Title VII is directed. 42 U.S.C. §2000e-2(a). Insofar as §704(a) expressly protects employees from retaliation for filing a "charge" under Title VII, and a charge under §703(a) alleging unlawful discharge would necessarily be brought by a former employee, it is far more consistent to include former employees within the scope of "employees" protected by §704(a).

In further support of this view, petitioner argues that the word "employees" includes former employees because to hold otherwise would effectively vitiate much of the protection afforded by §704(a). See Brief for Petitioner 20-30. This is also the position taken by the EEOC. See Brief for United States and EEOC as *Amici Curiae* 16-25; see also 2 EEOC Compliance Manual §614.7(f). According to the EEOC, exclusion of former employees from the protection of §704(a) would undermine the effectiveness of Title VII by allowing the threat of postemployment retaliation to deter victims of discrimination from complaining to the EEOC, and would provide a perverse incentive for employers to fire employees who might bring Title VII claims. Brief for United States and EEOC as *Amici Curiae* 18-21.

Those arguments carry persuasive force given their coherence and their consistency with a primary purpose of antiretaliation provisions: Maintaining unfettered access to statutory remedial mechanisms. *Cf. NLRB v. Scrivener*, 405 U.S. 117, 121-122, 31 L. Ed. 2d 79, 92 S. Ct. 798 (1972) (National Labor Relations Act); *Mitchell v. Robert DeMario Jewelry, Inc.*, 361 U.S. 288, 292-293, 4 L. Ed. 2d 323, 80 S. Ct. 332 (1960) (Fair Labor Standards Act). The EEOC quite persuasively maintains that it would be destructive of this purpose of the antiretaliation provision for an employer to be able to retaliate with impunity against an entire class of acts under Title VII — for example, complaints regarding discriminatory termination. We agree with these contentions and find that they support the inclusive interpretation of "employees" in §704(a) that is already suggested by the broader context of Title VII.

III

We hold that the term "employees," as used in §704(a) of Title VII, is ambiguous as to whether it includes former employees. It being more consistent with the broader context of Title VII and the primary purpose of §704(a), we hold that former employees are included within §704(a)'s coverage. Accordingly, the decision of the Fourth Circuit is reversed.

It is so ordered.

▶ Appendix D: Sample Documents

Employment Reference Check

Basic Form

At a minimum, the questions on the following form should be asked for all positions, even when a previous employer has indicated that only limited information can be provided. Even if a previous employer refuses to answer these specific questions, an employer can still show that it attempted to obtain this information. This may be critical, especially in defending against allegations of negligent hiring. Additional reference questions (which may be appropriate for more senior positions) are included at Appendix D.

Name: *Julie Burkhart*

Position: *Customer Service Representative*

Company: *Eastern Allied Services*

Phone: *884-3011*

Individual spoken to: *Jane Funkhouser*

Verified employment dates: ✔ Yes _____ No

If no, the correct dates: _____ to _____

Verified the position held: ✔ Yes _____ No

If no, the correct position: _____

Has he/she ever been warned or discharged for absenteeism, tardiness or failure to notify your company when absent? _____ Yes ✔ No

Has he/she ever been warned or discharged for theft? _____ Yes ✔ No

Has he/she ever been warned or discharged for sexual harassment, fighting, assault or other related offenses, or for violating safety rules? _____ Yes ✔ No

Do you have any reason to believe that he/she poses a risk in a work environment of violence, abuse, or harassment? _____ Yes ✔ No

Note: You may have a legal obligation to disclose this.

If given the opportunity, would you rehire? ✔ Yes _____ No

Comments: _____

Employment Reference Check
Reference Check of Applicant

First – Ask All References to Keep This Confidential!

	Reference #1	**Reference #2**
How do you know APPLICANT? When was the last time you had contact with him/her? How l known him/her?		
In what way have you had the opportunity to evaluate the work of APPLICANT? How often have you had the chance to evaluate his work?		
Have you seen only his finished product or have you actually worked with him/her?		
How would you describe APPLICANT's *communication skills* (verbal, written, listening)? Can you give me specific descriptors and examples? Is this a key strength, adequate skill or something he/she can work on?		
How would you describe APPLICANT's *creative thinking/problem solving skills*? Can you give me specific descriptors and examples? Is this a key strength, adequate skill or something he/she can work on?		
How would you describe APPLICANT's *effectiveness in helping others*? Can you give me specific descriptors and examples? Is this a key strength, adequate skill or something he/she can work on?		
How would you describe APPLICANT's *ability to maintain a positive approach in the face of conflict or diversity*? Can you give me specific descriptors and examples? Is this a key strength, adequate skill or something he/she can work on?		
How does APPLICANT *respond to supervision*? What type of supervisor would APPLICANT work especially well with?		

(continued)

Employment Reference Check

Reference Check of Applicant

	Reference #1	Reference #2
How does APPLICANT react when his decisions are challenged?		
Describe APPLICANT's business knowledge and his/her ability to understand complex business issues? Can you give me specific descriptors and examples? Is this a key strength, adequate skill or something he/she can work on?		
Describe APPLICANT's *ability to make effective presentations to small or large groups and/or coworkers or senior leaders.* Can you give me specific descriptors and examples? Is this a key strength, adequate skill or something he/she can work on?		
Describe APPLICANT's *ability to put ego aside and be open-minded.* Can you give me specific descriptors and examples? Is this a key strength, adequate skill or something to work on?		
Describe APPLICANT's *ability to manage himself/herselfself and others while working on multiple projects.* Can you give me specific descriptors and examples? Is this a key strength, adequate skill or something to work on?		
Describe APPLICANT's *maturity.* Can you give me specific descriptors and examples? Is this a key strength, adequate skill or something to work on?		
All of us have development needs and one of the qualities that Employer admires about people is their ability to continue to develop weaknesses. If there was one thing APPLICANT could work on to be even more effective, what would it be?		
What qualities would an individual need to work with APPLICANT?		

(continued)

Employment Reference Check

Reference Check of Applicant

	Reference #1	**Reference #2**
What environment does APPLICANT thrive in?		
Has APPLICANT ever been warned or discharged for sexual harassment, fighting, assault or other related offenses, or convicted of a crime?		
Do you have any reason to believe that he/she poses a risk of violence, abuse, or harassment in a work environment?		
Do you know whether APPLICANT has ever been terminated, disciplined in the performance of his duties or warned about the performance of his duties?		
What level of management is APPLICANT capable of?		
Why do you think APPLICANT is successful?		
Does anything stand out regarding his/her work performance?		
How would he/she handle the transition to a much smaller organization?		
Is there anyone else that I could contact to answer these questions?		

<u>**Training Exercise**</u>

Maintaining Personnel Files

The following is a *mock* personnel file. It is very similar in many ways to personnel files as they are maintained by most employers. Working alone, in pairs or in small groups, determine what documentation should be removed from the personnel file and what should be maintained. If you are working with others, discuss your reasoning for removing or maintaining each document. You may refer to the answer key provided. When your review is complete, compare your results with the list in Chapter 4 of what should properly be removed from the file.

You have been asked to review your company's personnel files and to discard any material that should not be included in the files. After reading the preceding discussion, remove all items from Julie Burkhart's personnel file that should be destroyed, or filed separately from the personnel files. An answer key is provided at the end of the file. (Please note, the forms included may or may not be legally correct. Do not rely on these forms for specific application or use. They are included as part of this training resource only for instructional purposes.)

Sample Personnel File

ABC
Application for Employment

ABC values a diverse workforce and is in principle, as well as in practice, an equal opportunity employer. Applicants are considered for all positions without regard to race, color, religion, gender, national origin, ancestry, age, marital or veteran status, pregnancy or disability. (Accommodations can and will be made in accordance with the Americans with Disabilities Act.)

Receipt of this application does not imply that you will be employed. Our company considers you an applicant only for the specific position(s) you are applying for. We do not accept applications that fail to designate specific positions. Your application will be considered "active" until the position for which you are applying has been filled, or for 60 days, whichever is sooner. If you are hired, proof of citizenship or immigration status will be required upon employment. Fingerprints and pre-employment checks may also be required.

Last Name	First	Middle	Date
Burkhart	*Julie*	*Lynn*	*3/12/90*

Street Address	Social Security Number
13653 Roosevelt Dr.	*298-78-0244*

City	State	Zip	Home Telephone
Marlington	*OH*	*92376*	*(555) 867-5309*

Specific Positions Applying For:		Salary Requirements:
1. *Customer Service* 2.		$ *Negotiable*

Who referred you to us for employment?	Date available:	Available for:
Olivia Bugansky	*4/1/90*	[X] Full time [ ] Part time [ ] Shift Work [ ] Temporary

Have you filed an application here before?   [ ] Yes [X] No   If yes, when?

Have you any relatives or close friends employed by ABC or any affiliate?   [ ] Yes [X] No

If so, state name and relationship and affiliate:_____

Have you been employed by ABC or any of its affiliates previously?   [ ] Yes [X] No

If yes, give dates: From   To

Are you prevented from lawfully becoming employed in this country because of visa or immigration status?   [ ] Yes [X] No

(Proof of citizenship or immigration status will be required upon hire.)

Have you ever been convicted, pleaded guilty or no contest to a felony or other criminal offense involving   dishonesty or breach of trust which has not been annulled or expunged (including, but not limited to robbery, embezzlement, forgery, perjury, tax evasion)?

[ ] Yes [X] No   (Conviction will not necessarily disqualify an applicant from employment.) If so, explain in detail.

(continued)

If you have any work experience or special training in any of the following areas, please check:

_____ Credit Analysis	_____ Auditing
_____ Paralegal	_____ Accounting
_____ Shorthand _____ w.p.m.	**X** Calculator/Adding Machine
_____ Typewriter _____ w.p.m.	_____ Accounts Payable/Receivable
X Word Processing **83** w.p.m.	_____ Machine Transcription
X Filing	**X** Software: **Word, Lotus**
_____ CRT	**X** PC

EDUCATION (You may include training received in the military if applicable.)

Name and Address of School	Years Completed	Degree/Diploma	Course of Study	G.P.A.
High School *Marlboro*	9 10 11 (12)	*Diploma*	*General*	*3.8*
Business Trade/Tech School	1 2 3 4			
College *Phillips University*	1 2 3 (4)	*B.A.*	*English*	*3.6*
Graduate School	1 2 3 4			

List scholastic honors, offices held and activities in High School/College/Graduate School that you feel would be beneficial in the performance of the job you have applied for (memberships which would reveal sex, race, religion, national origin, age, ancestry, disability, military, or other protected status may be excluded):

_____

REFERENCES

List References Who Are Not Former Employers or Friends				
Name	Address	Telephone Number	Profession or Position	How Long Known
Dana Carroll	*6 McAlinden St. Bridgetown, WA 03662*	*(555)499-1415*	*Sales Rep*	*6 years*
Travis Goldberg	*1378 Hayden Ave. Colton, OH 57901*	*(555)212-6254*	*Professor*	*9 years*
Jayne Hopkins	*594 Brittany Dr. Markel, PA 77506*	*(555)569-5712*	*Graphic Designer*	*4 years*

PREVIOUS EMPLOYMENT (Most Recent First)

Dates From: Mo./Yr.	To: Mo./Yr.	Employer (Full Name and Address)	Nature of Duties	Rate	Immediate Supervisor	Reason for Leaving
5/86	*Current*	*Eastern Allied Services 47 Hiram Ct Markel, PA 77506*	*Customer Service Rep.*		*Jane Funkhouser*	*Moving*
8/83	*5/86*	*The Sign Shop 1900 Edison Ave. Taylor, PA 77505*	*Receptionist*		*Terren Frenz*	*Better pay*
9/79	*8/83*	*Frontier Tavern 314 Maple St. Sexton, OH 57912*	*Server*		*Carol Brant*	*Better position*

If presently employed, why do you desire to change your place of employment? *I will be moving 3/26/90.*

Have you ever been disciplined, discharged, or asked to resign? ☐ Yes ☒ No   If so, explain. _____

(This will not necessarily disqualify an applicant from employment.)

(continued)

UNEMPLOYMENT RECORD

Account for all periods of unemployment of two week's duration or more during the past two years. (Periods of unemployment which would reveal a disability may be excluded.)

From (Month/Year)	To (Month/Year)	State what you were doing

APPLICANT'S STATEMENT AND RELEASE

PLEASE READ CAREFULLY BEFORE SIGNING. IF YOU HAVE ANY QUESTIONS REGARDING THIS STATEMENT, PLEASE ASK THE EMPLOYMENT INTERVIEWER BEFORE SIGNING.

TRUTH

I certify that the information provided in this application is true and complete to the best of my knowledge. I understand that the employer is relying on my complete honesty. I understand that any inaccuracy, misrepresentation, or incomplete answer provided by me in this application will cancel the application or may result in termination, if I have been employed.

INVESTIGATION

I hereby authorize ABC to conduct an investigation to obtain any requested information and to investigate all statements made by me in this application. I hereby direct former employers, all references, and all applicable government agencies to respond to ABC's questions concerning my application for employment. I understand that the information released or provided is for business use by the company and may be disclosed to third parties as necessary in the conduct of its business. If I am hired, I authorize ABC to supply my employment record, in whole or in part, to any prospective employer, government agency, or other party with a legal and proper interest. I release ABC, these parties and any individual, including record custodians, from any and all liability for any damage that may result from furnishing the requested information or any of my personal records.

EMPLOYMENT AT WILL

I understand that if I am employed by ABC, I will be an employee at will. My employment can be terminated at any time by me or ABC, with or without notice, and with or without reason, in accordance with the laws of the State of Ohio. Any oral statements or promises to the contrary are not binding on ABC. If hired, I will comply with all rules and regulations of ABC.

3/12/90	*Julie Burkhart*
Date	Signature

(continued)

APPLICANT'S DISCLOSURE AND RELEASE

<u>A Consumer Report may be obtained for employment purposes</u>

I understand that the Company may obtain a consumer report, including an investigative consumer report, containing information as to my credit worthiness, credit standing and credit capacity, character, general reputation, personal characteristics and mode of living. Should the Company request an investigative consumer report, I recognize that I have the right to demand, upon written request, a complete and accurate disclosure of the nature and scope of the investigation and a written summary of my rights under the Fair Credit Reporting Act.

My signature below authorizes the Company to obtain a consumer report, including an investigative consumer report, for employment purposes as part of the pre-employment background investigation and at any time during employment, if I am hired.

Julie Burkhart   *3/12/90*

Signature of Applicant   Date

U.S. Department of Justice
Immigration and Naturalization Service

OMB No. 1115-0136
Employment Eligibility Verification

Please read instructions carefully before completing this form. The instructions must be available during completion of this form. **ANTI-DISCRIMINATION NOTICE.** It is illegal to discriminate against work eligible individuals. Employers **CANNOT** specify which document(s) they will accept from an employee. The refusal to hire an individual because of a future expiration date may also constitute illegal discrimination.

Section 1. Employee Information and Verification. To be completed and signed by employee at the time employment begins

Print Name: Last	First	Middle Initial	Maiden Name
Burkhart	Julie	L.	Ramsey

Address (Street Name and Number)	Apt. #	Date of Birth (month/day/year)
13653 Roosevelt Dr.		1/22/61

City	State	Zip Code	Social Security #
Marlington	OH	92376	298-78-0244

I am aware that federal law provides for imprisonment and/or fines for false statements or use of false documents in connection with the completion of this form.

I attest, under penalty of perjury, that I am (check one of the following):
☒ A citizen or national of the United States
☐ A Lawful Permanent Resident (Alien # A _____)
☐ An alien authorized to work until ___/___/___
(Alien # or Admission # _____)

Employee's Signature	Date (month/day/year)
Julie Burkhart	3/12/90

Preparer and/or Translator Certification. (To be completed and signed if Section 1 is prepared by a person other than the employee.) I attest, under penalty of perjury, that I have assisted in the completion of this form and that to the best of my knowledge the information is true and correct.

Preparer's/Translator's Signature	Print Name

Address (Street Name and Number, City, State, Zip Code)	Date (month/day/year)

Section 2. Employer Review and Verification. To be completed and signed by employer. Examine one document from List A OR examine one document from List B **and** one from List C as listed on the reverse of this form and record the title, number and expiration date, if any, of the document(s)

	List A	OR	List B	AND	List C
Document title:	Passport				
Issuing authority:	US Govt				
Document #:	9147569325				
Expiration Date (if any):	2/29/96		___/___/___		___/___/___
Document #:					
Expiration Date (if any):	___/___/___				

CERTIFICATION - I attest, under penalty of perjury, that I have examined the document(s) presented by the above-named employee, that the above-listed document(s) appear to be genuine and to relate to the employee named, that the employee began employment on (month/day/year) 3/12/90 and that to the best of my knowledge the employee is eligible to work in the United States. (State employment agencies may omit the date the employee began employment).

Signature of Employer or Authorized Representative	Print Name	Title
Lance Schulz	Lance Schulz	VP-Human Resources

Business or Organization Name	Address (Street Name and Number, City, State, Zip Code)	Date (month/day/year)
ABC Organization		3/12/90

Section 3. Updating and Reverification. To be completed and signed by employer

A. New Name (if applicable)	B. Date of rehire (month/day/year) (if applicable)

C. If employee's previous grant of work authorization has expired, provide the information below for the document that establishes current employment eligibility.

Document Title: _____ Document #: _____ Expiration Date (if any): ___/___/___

I attest, under penalty of perjury, that to the best of my knowledge, this employee is eligible to work in the United States, and if the employee presented document(s), the document(s) I have examined appear to be genuine and to relate to the individual.

Signature of Employer or Authorized Representative	Date (month/day/year)

Form I-9 (Rev. 11-21-91) N

Employee Acknowledgement of Receipt of Handbook

This Employee Handbook contains policies and procedures that ABC ("Company") expects all employees to read, understand and follow. The policies and procedures set forth in this Handbook are intended as guidelines only and are subject to change at the sole discretion of the Company (except that the at-will employment policy as set forth will not change). Changes to this Handbook may be made only by Company in writing. Changes and updates will be communicated to each employee and will become a part of this Handbook. In the event of any contradictions between the contents of the Handbook and practice, the Handbook applies. I understand that this Handbook is the property of Company, and, upon termination of employment, I agree to return this Handbook to my supervisor. I also agree not to make copies of the Handbook or any part of the Handbook. This Handbook supersedes any previous handbook or unwritten policies.

At-Will Employment

This Handbook should not be construed as, and is not intended as, a contract guaranteeing employment for any specified duration. All employees are employees at will in accordance with applicable laws. This means that I am free to terminate employment at any time, for any reason, and the Company retains that same right. The decision to discharge remains within the sole discretion of the Company. Nothing in this Handbook modifies the employment-at-will relationship or creates any contract of employment, either express or implied.

I understand that, while Company managers or officers have the authority to hire me, they do not have the authority to promise employment for any specific amount of time, or to make any promises or commitments contrary to the foregoing. No Company manager, supervisor, or representative other than the President has the authority to enter into such an agreement with me. Moreover, any such agreement with the Company shall not be enforceable unless it is in writing.

Trade Secrets/Non-Competes

I agree not to bring or use any trade secret, confidential or proprietary information from prior employers to my new position. I agree that I am not subject to any covenant not-to-compete agreement or any other work-restricting agreement. I agree to indemnify and hold the Company harmless for any damages and legal expenses in the event that this representation and warranty is false.

I have read, understand, and acknowledge the foregoing. I also acknowledge that I have received a copy of the Company Handbook, including the Harassment policy, and that I may discuss any items for which I have questions or comments at any time with my supervisor.

Julie Burkhart	*3/12/90*
Employee's Signature	Date

ABC Organization
Voluntary Self-Identification Survey

ABC Organization is a federal government contractor. As a matter of company policy as well as applicable law, we are required to keep records and perform certain analyses of our employee pool by race, ethnicity and gender. Since such analyses are only possible if we know the EEO profile of our employees, we are using this survey and ask that you return it to us promptly.

The categories listed below are those used by the U.S. Bureau of Census and Department of Labor and are the only options available for Federal reporting purposes.

Circle One

Circle One Only

Male

White, not of Hispanic Origin (includes Middle East)

Female

Black

Hispanic (all races)

Asian or Pacific Islander

American Indian, Eskimo or Aleut

Name *Julie Burkhart* Zip Code *92376*

County and State of Residence *Wood, Ohio*

ABC Organization
Request for Family or Medical Leave or Personal Leave

PLEASE PRINT

Request for Family or Medical Leave or Personal Leave must be made, if practical, at least thirty (30) days prior to the date the requested leave is to begin.

Name: _____*Julie Burkhart*_____ Date: ___*8/14/93*___ Status: _____

___*X*___ Full-Time _____ Part-Time _____ Temporary

Length of Service: ___*3 years*___ Hire Date: ___*3/12/90*___

I request Family or Medical Leave or Personal Leave for one or more of the following reasons:

Family and Medical Leave

_____ Because of the birth of my child in order to care for him or her.

        Expected date of birth   ____ / ____ / ____

        Leave to start   ____ / ____ / ____

        Actual date of birth   ____ / ____ / ____

        Expected return date   ____ / ____ / ____

_____ Because of the placement of a child with me for adoption or foster care.

        Date of placement   ____ / ____ / ____

        Leave to start   ____ / ____ / ____

        Expected return date   ____ / ____ / ____

___*X*___ In order to care for my spouse, child or parent who has a serious health condition.*

        Leave to start   *9* / *23* / *93*

        Expected return date   *10* / *6* / *93*

_____ For a serious health condition* that makes me unable to perform my duties. Describe:

        Leave to start   ____ / ____ / ____

        Expected return date   ____ / ____ / ____

---

* A physician's certification is required for leave due to a serious health condition. Failure to provide the required certification may result in disciplinary measures. Recertification is requested every thirty (30) days unless your initial certification provides for a longer period of incapacity.

(continued)

Personal Leave

_____ For other reasons. Describe: _____

_____

Leave to start   _____ / _____ / _____
Expected return date   _____ / _____ / _____

_____ Requested intermittent leave schedule (only applicable for medical leaves)

_____

_____

Have you taken Family or Medical Leave in the past twelve (12) months?   Yes _____ No **X**

If "Yes", how many workdays? _____

Have you taken a Personal Leave in the past twelve (12) months?   Yes **X** No _____

If "Yes", how many workdays? _____ *3* _____

If my leave is Family or Medical Leave and not Personal Leave, I understand and agree to the following provisions:

- Upon my return following a Family or Medical Leave, I am entitled to restoration to my same or an equivalent job, with no loss of accrued benefits.

- I have worked for ABC Organization for at least twelve (12) months (need not be consecutive) and at least 1,250 hours in the previous twelve (12) months.

- Leave taken as Family and Medical Leave will count towards my annual Family or Medical Leave entitlement.

- This Leave will be unpaid or, in the case of my own disability, payment will occur under a company disability insurance plan if I am so covered.

- I will be required to first exhaust my paid sick leave as part of my twelve (12) weeks of Leave.

- After twelve (12) weeks of Leave, if I do not return to work or contact my supervisor or manager on the date intended, I will be considered to have abandoned my job.

- ABC may require medical certification that the Leave is needed due to my serious health condition or that of a family member. ABC may also, at its expense, require a second medical opinion. If the first and second opinions differ, ABC may request a third medical opinion, also at its expense, which is then binding.

- If I fail to return to work after the Leave for reasons other than the continuation, recurrence or onset of a serious health condition that would entitle me to Medical Leave or other circumstances beyond my control, I will be financially responsible for the medical insurance premiums ABC paid while I was on Leave, or for my share of any non-health benefit premiums ABC paid while I was on Leave.

(continued)

- I will be required to provide a fitness-for-duty certificate to return to my employment. If I do not, my return to work may be delayed.

- I agree that health care providers may provide information to ABC for purposes of determining my eligibility for Leave.

- I agree that falsification of this document, or falsely obtaining Leave, will result in discipline, up to and including termination.

Employee Signature: _____*Julie Burkhart*_____ Date: _8_ / _14_ / _93_

Evaluation Form

Please respond to each applicable item by placing a ✔ in the appropriate category.

Employee Name *Julie Burkhart*

Date of Evaluation *3/12/99*

Competence, Quality of Work, Work Habits	Excellent	Satisfactory	Needs Improvement*	Unsatisfactory*
1. General Knowledge of the Job	☐	✔	☐	☐
2. Analytical Ability, Decision-Making Skills (ability to gather facts and examine issues)	☐	✔	☐	☐
3. Thoroughness, Attention to Detail, Accuracy	☐	☐	✔	☐
4. Writing Ability	☐	✔	☐	☐
5. Oral Ability	☐	✔	☐	☐
6. Quality of Work (caliber of work produced on a consistent basis)	☐	☐	✔	☐
7. Judgment	☐	✔	☐	☐
8. Initiative, Creativity	☐	✔	☐	☐
9. Timeliness	☐	☐	✔	☐
10. Organizational Skills, Time Management	☐	✔	☐	☐
11. Response Under Pressure	☐	✔	☐	☐
12. Efficiency	☐	☐	✔	☐
13. Supervisory Ability, Leadership	☐	✔	☐	☐
14. Willingness to Accept Supervision and Criticism	☐	✔	☐	☐
15. Diligence and Dependability	☐	☐	✔	☐

To: Tricia Theaker
Re: Performance Evaluation
From: Julie Burkhart

    I do not agree with my last evaluation. My old supervisor felt my performance was fine. I had no problems. Now, the new supervisor is unrealistic in her expectations. Also, we have fewer people in our department, so I am expected to do more. She does not understand the amount of work that I have. It is impossible to do any more than I have been. Also, since I complained about her treatment of me, I think she treats me more harshly than other employees.

Evaluation Form

Employee Name ___Julie Burkhart___

Date of Evaluation ___3/10/98___

Please respond to each applicable item by placing a ✔ in the appropriate category.

Competence, Quality of Work, Work Habits	Excellent	Satisfactory	Needs Improvement*	Unsatisfactory*
1. General Knowledge of the Job	☐	✔	☐	☐
2. Analytical Ability, Decision-Making Skills (ability to gather facts and examine issues)	☐	✔	☐	☐
3. Thoroughness, Attention to Detail, Accuracy	☐	✔	☐	☐
4. Writing Ability	☐	☐	✔	☐
5. Oral Ability	☐	✔	☐	☐
6. Quality of Work (caliber of work produced on a consistent basis)	☐	✔	☐	☐
7. Judgment	☐	✔	☐	☐
8. Initiative, Creativity	☐	☐	✔	☐
9. Timeliness	☐	✔	☐	☐
10. Organizational Skills, Time Management	☐	✔	✔	☐
11. Response Under Pressure	☐	✔	☐	☐
12. Efficiency	☐	✔	✔	☐
13. Supervisory Ability, Leadership	☐	✔	☐	☐
14. Willingness to Accept Supervision and Criticism	☐	✔	☐	☐
15. Diligence and Dependability	☐	☐	✔	☐

Evaluation Form

Please respond to each applicable item by placing a ✔ in the appropriate category.

Employee Name *Julie Burkhart*

Date of Evaluation *4/10/97*

Competence, Quality of Work, Work Habits	Excellent	Satisfactory	Needs Improvement*	Unsatisfactory*
1. General Knowledge of the Job	☐	✔	☐	☐
2. Analytical Ability, Decision-Making Skills (ability to gather facts and examine issues)	☐	✔	☐	☐
3. Thoroughness, Attention to Detail, Accuracy	☐	☐	✔	☐
4. Writing Ability	☐	☐	✔	☐
5. Oral Ability	☐	☐	✔	☐
6. Quality of Work (caliber of work produced on a consistent basis)	☐	☐	✔	☐
7. Judgment	☐	✔	☐	☐
8. Initiative, Creativity	☐	✔	☐	☐
9. Timeliness	☐	☐	✔	☐
10. Organizational Skills, Time Management	☐	☐	✔	☐
11. Response Under Pressure	☐	✔	☐	☐
12. Efficiency	☐	✔	☐	☐
13. Supervisory Ability, Leadership	☐	☐	✔	☐
14. Willingness to Accept Supervision and Criticism	☐	☐	✔	☐
15. Diligence and Dependability	☐	☐	✔	☐

Evaluation Form

Employee Name ___Julie Burkhart___

Date of Evaluation ___2/29/96___

Please respond to each applicable item by placing a ✔ in the appropriate category.

Competence, Quality of Work, Work Habits	Excellent	Satisfactory	Needs Improvement*	Unsatisfactory*
1. General Knowledge of the Job	☐	✔	☐	☐
2. Analytical Ability, Decision-Making Skills (ability to gather facts and examine issues)	☐	☐	✔	☐
3. Thoroughness, Attention to Detail, Accuracy	☐	☐	✔	☐
4. Writing Ability	☐	☐	✔	☐
5. Oral Ability	☐	✔	☐	☐
6. Quality of Work (caliber of work produced on a consistent basis)	☐	✔	☐	☐
7. Judgment	☐	☐	✔	☐
8. Initiative, Creativity	☐	☐	✔	☐
9. Timeliness	☐	☐	✔	☐
10. Organizational Skills, Time Management	☐	✔	☐	☐
11. Response Under Pressure	☐	✔	☐	☐
12. Efficiency	☐	☐	✔	☐
13. Supervisory Ability, Leadership	☐	☐	✔	☐
14. Willingness to Accept Supervision and Criticism	☐	✔	☐	☐
15. Diligence and Dependability	☐	✔	☐	☐

Evaluation Form

Please respond to each applicable item by placing a ✔ in the appropriate category.

Employee Name __Julie Burkhart__

Date of Evaluation __3/10/95__

Competence, Quality of Work, Work Habits	Excellent	Satisfactory	Needs Improvement*	Unsatisfactory*
1. General Knowledge of the Job		✔		
2. Analytical Ability, Decision-Making Skills (ability to gather facts and examine issues)			✔	
3. Thoroughness, Attention to Detail, Accuracy		✔		
4. Writing Ability			✔	
5. Oral Ability			✔	
6. Quality of Work (caliber of work produced on a consistent basis)		✔		
7. Judgment			✔	
8. Initiative, Creativity		✔		
9. Timeliness		✔		
10. Organizational Skills, Time Management		✔		
11. Response Under Pressure		✔		
12. Efficiency			✔	
13. Supervisory Ability, Leadership		✔		
14. Willingness to Accept Supervision and Criticism		✔		
15. Diligence and Dependability		✔		

Evaluation Form

Please respond to each applicable item by placing a ✔ in the appropriate category.

Employee Name ___Julie Burkhart___

Date of Evaluation ___4/1/94___

Competence, Quality of Work, Work Habits	Excellent	Satisfactory	Needs Improvement*	Unsatisfactory*
1. General Knowledge of the Job	☐	✔	☐	☐
2. Analytical Ability, Decision-Making Skills (ability to gather facts and examine issues)	☐	✔	☐	☐
3. Thoroughness, Attention to Detail, Accuracy	☐	☐	✔	☐
4. Writing Ability	☐	☐	✔	☐
5. Oral Ability	☐	☐	✔	☐
6. Quality of Work (caliber of work produced on a consistent basis)	☐	☐	✔	☐
7. Judgment	☐	☐	✔	☐
8. Initiative, Creativity	☐	☐	✔	☐
9. Timeliness	☐	✔	☐	☐
10. Organizational Skills, Time Management	☐	✔	☐	☐
11. Response Under Pressure	☐	☐	✔	☐
12. Efficiency	☐	☐	✔	☐
13. Supervisory Ability, Leadership	☐	☐	✔	☐
14. Willingness to Accept Supervision and Criticism	☐	☐	✔	☐
15. Diligence and Dependability	☐	✔	☐	☐

SUBPOENA (INCLUDING DUCES TECUM COMMAND)

Hazard County Court of Common Pleas

Mr. Winn Bigg	Case No. _97-C688_
Plaintiff	
	Judge _Hand_
v.	
	Subpoena
ABC Corporation	☐ Provide Testimony
Defendant	☐ Duces Tecum

To: ___*Ms. Julie Burkhart*___

_____

_____

☐   **YOU ARE HEREBY COMMANDED** to appear in the Hazard County Court of Common Pleas, Courthouse, and give testimony in the above-referenced matter on the date and time and Courtroom noted below:

Date:	_7/11/98_
Time:	_2:00 p.m._
Courtroom Number:	_4_

☐   **YOU ARE HEREBY COMMANDED** to appear at the law offices of Doyle and Shields, 51 North Main Street, Suite 333, and give testimony in the above-referenced matter on the date and time noted below:

Date:	_____
Time:	_____

☐   **YOU ARE HEREBY COMMANDED** to produce for inspection and copying the following documents or things at the place, date and time specified below:

Documents:	_____
	_____
Place:	_____
Date:	_____
Time:	_____

Date: _____*7/3/98*_____ , 1998

Respectfully submitted,

Molly K. Doyle

Workers' Compensation Accident Investigation Report

PART 1   IDENTIFICATION INFORMATION

Employee Name *Julie Burkhart*

Date of Accident *February 14* , 20 *00* Time *9:30*   (AM) PM

Occupation *Customer Service*   Shift *1st*

Department *Sales*   ID *7311*

PART 2   SUPPLEMENTARY INFORMATION

Company *ABC Organization*

Mailing Address

City	State	Zip Code

Telephone (   )

Establishment of Location (if different from above) *corporate offices*

Accident Location   ☒ Same as establishment?   ☒ On premises? (Check if applies)

Risk No.   Manual(s)   Claim No.

Employee Address

City	State	Zip Code

Telephone (   )

Sex   Age   Date of Birth   SSN

Was Injured Person Performing Regular Job at Time of Accident?   ☒ Yes   ☐ No

Length of Service: With Employer *10 years*   On this job *10 years*

Time Shift Started *8:00*   (AM) PM   Overtime?   ☐ Yes   ☒ No

Name and address of Physician *Dr. Brendan O'Malley*

City	State	Zip Code

If Hospitalized, Name and Address of Hospital *N/A*

City	State	Zip Code

Fatality?   ☐ Yes   ☒ No   If yes, Date of Death

(If Death, Attach Coroner's Report)

© Thompson Publishing Group, Inc.

Dear Mr. Koprivnikar,

May I have next Tuesday off please? My church is having a full-day service to celebrate the Feast of Saint Carmelina, an important patron saint of our religious order.

Thank you.

Julie Burkhart

Customer Service Comment Card

ABC Organization would like to recognize employees that go *"the extra mile"* and provide quality service.

Julie Burkhart
_____
Employee's Name

☒ Exceeded my expectations
☐ Met my expectations
☐ Fell short of my expectations

Please Explain: *I had a problem with an invoice. I spoke to Ms. Burkhart and she immediately corrected the problem. She is very friendly & courteous!*

Date: *12/13/99*
Name: *Janet Rawlings*
Address: *3729 Willow Lane*
City *Toledo* State *OH* Zip *43613*
Daytime Telephone Number *(419) 555-6932*

▲ **ABC Organization**

Customer Service Comment Card

ABC Organization would like to recognize employees that go *"the extra mile"* and provide quality service.

_____
Employee's Name

☐ Exceeded my expectations
☐ Met my expectations
☐ Fell short of my expectations

Please Explain: _____

Date: _____
Name: _____
Address: _____
City _____ State _____ Zip _____
Daytime Telephone Number _____

▲ **ABC Organization**

Customer Service Comment Card

ABC Organization would like to recognize employees that go *"the extra mile"* and provide quality service.

Julie Burkhart
_____
Employee's Name

☒ Exceeded my expectations
☐ Met my expectations
☐ Fell short of my expectations

Please Explain: *I went from being very annoyed to having confidence in your company again. What a joy to talk to Ms. Burkhart!*

Date: *11-10-99*
Name: *Amanda Boham*
Address: *155 Stony Oak Ln*
City *Toledo* State *OH* Zip *43623*
Daytime Telephone Number *(419) 155-0909*

▲ **ABC Organization**

Customer Service Comment Card

ABC Organization would like to recognize employees that go *"the extra mile"* and provide quality service.

Julie Burkhart
_____
Employee's Name

☒ Exceeded my expectations
☐ Met my expectations
☐ Fell short of my expectations

Please Explain: *I had several questions about an invoice. She was very helpful and patient!*

Date: *1/14/00*
Name: *Kim White*
Address: *520 Rutledge Ct.*
City *Toledo* State *OH* Zip *43614*
Daytime Telephone Number *(419) 893-4718*

▲ **ABC Organization**

in recognition of accomplishments for exceeding

company expectations

presents this award to

Julie Burkhart

Excellence Award

Tanya Houser

signature

January 22, 1993

date

Answer Key to Training Exercise

The following items should be removed from Julie Burkhart's personnel file. They may need to be maintained elsewhere, but not in the personnel file.

I-9:

Should be separately maintained, it may indicate race, national origin or ancestry.

Reference Checking Form:

This is not harmful but is unnecessary. Records concerning hiring decisions need only be maintained for one year after the decision is made.

Voluntary Self-Identification Survey:

This affirmative action document should not be included in the personnel file since it specifically concerns information about race, national origin and ancestry.

Request for Family or Medical Leave or Personal Leave:

This should be filed separately, as it may include information regarding a disability.

Evaluation Forms:

Only the most recent, or at most, the two most recent forms should be included.
Note from Julie Burkhart to Tricia Theaker regarding Performance Evaluation.
An employee's self-serving comments, which may weaken an employer's justification for adverse action, should never be a part of official company records.

Evaluation:

An employee's self-serving comments, which may weaken an employer's justification for adverse action, should never be a part of official company records.

Subpoena:

This may be evidence of an employee's participation activity and should not be maintained as a part of the personnel file.

The University of Knowledge Certificate:

This certificate could be included or records of training can be centrally maintained. It is not harmful to have it in a personnel file, but it is unnecessary unless it is required certification for this job.

Request for day off for religious holiday:

This is evidence of religious accommodation and should not be included.

Customer Service Comment Cards:

These comments should be acknowledged but not maintained by the employer as part of the personnel files.

Workers' Compensation Accident Investigation Report:

This is evidence of protected activity and should not be included.

Excellence Award:

This award should be recognized but not maintained by the employer as part of the personnel files.

Sample Complaint Form

The following is a sample complaint form that could be used to record an alleged victim's complaint about retaliation (or harassment or discrimination). No form is necessary, however, and a handwritten statement or blank paper can serve the same purpose, as long as all relevant information is included. Note that questions two through four will help the employer to determine the existence and identity of potential witnesses. Most importantly, note the statement at the end of the complaint, stating that the account is complete. This is extremely important and the employer should make sure the complaining party has provided a complete account.

Complaining Employee

1. Name:_____

2. Position: _____

3. Department/Shift:_____

4. Immediate Supervisor: _____

5. Filed prior complaint(s)?_____

Alleged Perpetrator [Where more than one alleged perpetrator, provide information on separate page.]

1. Name:_____

2. Position:_____

3. Department/Shift:_____

4. Immediate Supervisor: _____

Complained-Of Actions

1. What happened? (Provide details of what, when, where, and who did what.)

2. Company supervisors or co-workers who witnessed the complained-of actions:

(continued)

3.   Company supervisors or co-workers with whom you have discussed the complained- of actions:

4.   Non-employee witnesses of the complained-of actions:

5.   What would you like the Company to do to help you?

6.   Other information that could assist in the Company's investigation of this matter:

The above and any attached pages include all incidents and actions and constitute my complete complaint.

_____   _____

Complaining Employee's Signature   Date

Sworn to before me and subscribed in my presence this_____ day of_____ , 20___ .

Notary Public

Sample Investigation Report

These are actual notes taken by a human resources officer to document her investigation of allegations of sexual harassment. (All names have been changed.) Her investigation and notes were so thorough that they were referred to by the judge in an opinion that completely absolved the employer of any liability, even when it was quite likely that some harassment occurred. Her notes helped establish that the employer took all reasonable precautions, was thorough in its investigation and took action to prevent the conduct from occurring again. Note that she never uses the word "harassment." Although these notes deal with a harassment complaint, the format would be the same for a claim of retaliation or discrimination.

RE: Investigation Notes

Investigator: Melanie Right, Corporate Human Resources

June 15, 1998:

I investigated a complaint about Rich Brown. The complaint was made by Katherine Stewart ("Kathy"). Prior to the start of the investigation, I learned that the complaint was actually brought to the attention of the plant's human resource representative, Ellen Smith, on June 8, 1998, but was not reported to the president, Joe Boss, until Kathy did not return to work after taking a few vacation days, at which time Ellen decided to inform Joe of the situation. At this time, Joe and I made plans to meet with the employees involved the next day.

We first met with Kathy Stewart. I thanked her for meeting with us and explained that we would like her to share with us the entire situation that caused her to bring the complaint to our attention. She was very calm and was able to express herself very well. Her complaint involved the following:

1) She said that Rich would look at her legs and that this made her uncomfortable. She said she would pull herself totally up to the desk so her legs wouldn't show.

2) She said that Rich would touch her knee and sometimes let his hand linger on her knee (she demonstrated this for us, which appeared to be less than a second). She also said that on three different occasions, Rich had trapped her with his body in the conference room. This trapping was described by Kathy as if she was sitting at a desk and that Rich would be behind her with his arms each touching a different side of the desk so she couldn't move. She also said that Rich would touch her during conversations (touching her on the arm).

3) She said that Rich was possessive about her and would follow her when she went to other parts of the building. She even said he followed her to the restroom once. She also said that Rich would wait for her at the end of the day to walk her to her car. This made her uncomfortable.

4) She also said Rich made a big deal about her name and that this made her uncomfortable. He asked her if she wanted to be called Katherine or Kathy. Rich called her Katherine and seemed upset when a client called her Kathy.

5) She said that Rich would make comments to her and about her that made her feel uncomfortable. Kathy also said he referred to her as the "brains of the department and the looks too." This comment was said to Mike Willis and Kathy said that this made her feel like she was on

display and that it felt like that moment lasted an eternity (actually, it was just a one comment introduction).

6) She said that Rich had driven around her house. One day he remarked to her "I drove by your house last night." Kathy said she asked him why and that he said he just wanted to know where she lived.

7) She said Rich would tell her a lot of personal information about himself, his mother, father, wife, kids, stuff about high school, etc. He also asked Kathy if she dated a lot in high school. When Kathy said no and that she was still in the same relationship from high school, Rich commented "You're kidding, you mean he's the only guy you have ever been with."

I asked her if there was anything else that Rich did or had done that made her feel uncomfortable. She said no. I asked her if she had talked to anyone at the company about this. She detailed the following for Joe and me:

On June 7 she said she went to Bob Jones at his desk and told him everything she told us. He told her that she needed to go to Ellen Smith.

The next morning (June 8th at 7:55 am) she said she approached Ellen. She said she told her that he had been touching her and making her feel uncomfortable. She asked Ellen if she was being overly dramatic or was what she was experiencing not normal. Kathy said that Ellen suggested that she write Rich a letter and come right to the point that he was making her feel uncomfortable. Kathy said that Ellen told her not to talk to Rich and not to be alone with him in a room. I asked Kathy if she had told Ellen that she wanted to handle this herself without her help and if she was just going to her for advice (This is what Ellen had told me was the reason that she did not bring this to my or Joe's attention earlier). Kathy said she never told Ellen that she wanted to handle it on her own.

Kathy said she wrote the letter (we have a copy) and gave it to Rich Wednesday evening before she left for vacation. She said she told him to take the letter (sealed in an envelope) home for the weekend and read it and she left the room. Kathy went into a conference room. After reading the letter, Rich approached her and apologized repeatedly. He said he had no idea he was making her uncomfortable and that he had a pit in his stomach. She said he told her she was doing so well and wanted to know how he could make it up to her ... and that if he had increased her workload too much that they could discuss it ... and that he had gone to Joe to tell him what a great job she was doing. Kathy said she told Rich that this was not about her workload and that she wanted him to stop the sexual harassment.

She said that Ellen called her at home on Thursday evening and asked if she wanted to pursue this and make a formal complaint. Kathy said she felt dirty and disgusted and that she just wanted to escape. She said she was going to bed very early (9:00), not eating, and that she felt very depressed.

Tuesday morning, Kathy said that she called Rich's voice mail because she just couldn't handle coming back to work. Ellen then called Kathy and told her that she couldn't let this go on any further and that she had to tell Joe.

I asked Kathy if she had spoken to anyone else. She told us: That she had lunch with Bob Norris on Thursday and that she told him about it as a friend. She said he told her as a friend "not to run away". She also talked briefly with Ralph Jones.

Kathy told us that she just couldn't work with Rich again. That the sound of his voice repulsed her. She said she never had a problem with anyone else. We told her she would not have to work with Rich again and that we valued her as an employee. We assured her that we were taking this very seriously and she would not have to work with Rich again. I offered for her to be able to attend counseling sessions with a counselor of her choice during work time at the company's expense. I thanked her for speaking with us and told her that Joe or I would be available if she wanted to speak again. I did everything I could to put her at ease and thanked her for coming forward.

Next Joe and I talked to Ralph Jones. I told him that we needed to speak with him about a complaint that was very confidential. I asked him if he was aware of any information regarding a complaint about Rich Brown's behavior. He said that Kathy had seemed nervous and distracted and he asked her if something was wrong (this was Tuesday June 7th). She said that Rich was following her around. Ralph said he noticed several times that, if Kathy came upstairs, Rich would come up looking for her. He also said that Kathy said that Rich had touched her leg in his car and that he would call her at home relating to business. He also said that Kathy said that she would see his car around her house and that this made her uncomfortable. Ralph said he told her to contact Ellen Smith, and that if she didn't, he would. I asked Ralph if there was anything else about this situation that he hadn't already told us. He said no. I thanked him for speaking with us and asked him to keep our conversation confidential.

Next we spoke with Ellen Smith. We were concerned that Ellen knew about this situation last week. We asked her what happened and how she became aware. Ellen said that Kathy came into the office on Wednesday and said she had something to talk to her about. She said that Kathy said Rich Brown was making her feel uncomfortable ... grabbing her knee, possessive and touching her when they talked. Ellen said that Kathy's focus in talking with her was on whether she was being overdramatic about it. She said she didn't want to be a troublemaker or be responsible for anything bad happening to him, but that she just wanted to work. Ellen said she explained that if he was making her uncomfortable, she wasn't being overly dramatic. Ellen said she asked Kathy if she wanted Ellen to do anything and Kathy said no that she didn't want anything done, she wanted to take care of it herself. Ellen then suggested that Kathy could write him a letter and confront him about stopping the behavior. Ellen was adamant that Kathy did not want her involved further other than just giving her advice. Joe and I talked with Ellen and told her how important it is to follow up with the person making a complaint, even if the person says that they don't want you to. We told her how serious the mishandling of these situations can be and that it is her responsibility to act in the company's best interests (rather than just taking an employee counseling role). Ellen said that she understood and that she had learned something important from the situation.

Next Joe and I met with Rich. We talked to him outside of the office in a Conference Room at the Hilton Hotel. Rich was already on suspension, but we met with him to address the complaint in detail and get his response. Rich said that on Wednesday he had a meeting at 5:00 and he was getting ready to leave when Kathy handed him a letter. He said he thought it was going to be good news (a thank you for the opportunities he had given her). When he read the letter, he said he was shocked. He said he went to her and said he would never do anything to hurt her.

He said he told her "I have never touched you with sexual intent" and that he had even written a letter to Joe about how well she was doing. He said she seemed very satisfied and just said "Well, then we will just start fresh on Tuesday." He said she told him not to "change himself." I went through the details with Rich of Kathy's complaint (items 1-7 above under the Kathy conversation). Rich responded as follows:

1) He said he did not look at her like this.

2) He said he was a touchy person and that he touches guys and women when he talks to them. He said he has never put his hand on her leg.

3) He said this was very far-fetched. He said that he believes in always telling people where he is and that they should do the same in case an answer is needed on something. With regard to waiting for her to walk out at night, he said that she had told him she was worried about the safety of the parking lot and that he thought he was being thoughtful and a gentlemen.

4) He said he couldn't believe that this was an issue. He said that when she came into the department she told him that she liked to be introduced as Katherine in business settings. He told the clients that her name was Katherine. Then the clients called him and said what should we call her? "You told us her name was Katherine but she answers the phone Kathy." I wanted to go by her wishes so I asked her what name she wanted to be called.

5) He said he did say the "brains and looks" comment, but that this was meant to be complimentary and in good fun.

6) He said he did drive by her house because it was right on his way home. He reiterated that it was not out of his path and that he thought he might need to pick her up for work sometime.

7) He said that he didn't remember if he made this comment. He said that if he did, the intent was not sexual. He said if he said anything, he was simply referring to good long-term relationships like George and Amy Gant.

We told Rich that the complaint was very serious and we would be continuing our investigation. He said he had given this a great deal of thought and that his conscience was clear. He said he never intended to hurt anyone and that he had been working very hard to be more friendly with people since his change of responsibilities. He said he had received a lot of positive comments about the "new him." He said that Kathy's work was generally very good, but that if she would do something like this that he was worried about her emotional health. I asked Rich if there was anything else he wanted to tell us. He said no ... just that his conscience was clear. Joe told Rich we would be back in touch after we completed the investigation and that he was to regard this conversation as confidential.

Next, we received information from Ellen that there had been a previous complaint made about Rich by Ellen, Sally Kerns, and Alexis Todd and that this complaint had been addressed by Al Crawford, the prior president, many years earlier. We called Al and he said that it did occur about two or three years ago around Oct./Nov. 1996. He said that the complaint was about Rich making comments and telling stories and that there wasn't a complaint that he touched anybody. He said he remembered that Ellen had said he made a comment about his "manhood" around the copy machine. He said he addressed the complaint with Rich and no further comments were reported.

Conversation with Alexis Todd:

Joe and I spoke with Alexis in the conference room at the plant. I told her that we needed to speak with her about something very confidential and that we wanted her to be open and honest with us. I told her we had received a complaint about Rich Brown and asked if she had ever felt uncomfortable due to Rich's behavior or if she had witnessed or was aware of any situations about Rich and inappropriate conduct. Alexis said that Sally had come to her a couple years ago and wanted her to come forward and complain about Rich. Alexis told us that the president of the corporation knew about it. She said that one time Rich was fooling around and he sat in her lap. She said this was really no big deal, but that Sally wanted her to make a formal complaint. She said she talked to Ellen, and told Ellen that they didn't want anything to do with a formal complaint. Alexis said that the president was aware of this situation. She then told us that she knew about the complaint by Kathy. I asked her if there was anything else that she knew. She said no. We thanked her for talking with us and asked her to keep the conversation confidential. Conversation with Michelle Franks:

Joe and I spoke with Michelle in the conference room at the plant. I told her that we needed to speak with her about something very confidential and that we wanted her to be open and honest with us. I told her we had received a complaint about Rich Brown and asked if she had ever felt uncomfortable due to Rich's behavior or if she had witnessed or was aware of any situations about Rich and inappropriate behavior. Michelle said that "a couple of weeks ago, Kathy asked me to walk with her to her car. She said during the walk that Rich was making her feel uncomfortable calling her the 'looks of the department' and putting his hand on her knee." She said that later Kathy said that Ellen told her to keep track of things and dates about Rich. Michelle also told us that Kathy showed her the letter she was going to give to Rich. Michelle said she never witnessed the behavior between Rich and Kathy. I asked her if there was anything else that she knew. She said no. We thanked her for talking with us and asked her to keep the conversation confidential.

Conversation with Sally Kerns:

Joe and I spoke with Sally in the conference room at the plant. I told her that we needed to speak with her about something very confidential and that we wanted her to be open and honest with us. I told her we had received a complaint about Rich Brown and asked if she had ever felt uncomfortable due to Rich's behavior or if she had witnessed or was aware of any situations about Rich and inappropriate conduct. She became very upset immediately and could not hold back her anger. She said she couldn't believe this and that she didn't want to participate in this. She said she had made us aware of this before and that nothing happened. She said she had been through a terrible period dealing with this before and she wasn't willing to talk to us. She was very upset, loud and clearly irritated. I asked her when this had happened before and that Joe and I really wanted to know. She said that I had known of her previous complaint two years earlier because the president knew. I told her that Joe and I had not been involved and that if there had been a misunderstanding about a previous complaint that we didn't want that to happen again and would she please just talk with us. She said absolutely not, that she wouldn't and she left the conference room.

Conversation with Jenny Mitchell:

Joe and I spoke with Jenny in the conference room at the plant. I told her that we needed to speak with her about something very confidential and that we wanted her to be open and honest with us. I told her we had received a complaint about Rich Brown and asked if she had ever felt uncomfortable due to Rich's behavior or if she had witnessed or was aware of any situations about Rich and inappropriate conduct. She said she never witnessed any poor behavior by Rich. She said there had been a situation that made her upset about Sally. She told us that once when she, Rich and a few others were leaving work, Rich noticed that she had some loose hairs on her blouse (by her breast) and he twice (quickly) tried to take the hairs off of her blouse. She said she dealt with this on her own and that she did not feel the need to make any complaint. However, sometime after that, she said she told Sally about it. Then about a year later Sally came to her and told her that there was a harassment complaint brought against Rich and she wanted Jenny to come forward with the "hair on blouse" incident. Jenny said that this made her very upset and that she told Sally she didn't want to pursue it. She said she felt that Sally was going after Rich. She said she knew that Rich had made a comment to Ellen that embarrassed her. Jenny said she didn't see these things as sexual harassment and that she considers herself strong enough to deal with these little things on her own. I asked her again if she ever witnessed anything that she considered harassment by Rich Brown. She said no. I thanked her and explained that sexual harassment is "unwelcome behavior of a sexual nature" and that if Rich was making others feel uncomfortable with sexual comments or behavior that they had the right to bring it to our attention and ask for it to stop. Jenny said she understood. I asked her if there was anything else she wanted to tell us. She said no. I thanked her for speaking with us and asked her to keep our conversation confidential.

Conversation with Bob Norris:

Joe and I spoke with Bob in the conference room in the plant. I told him that we needed to speak with him about something very confidential and that we wanted him to be open and honest with us. I told him we had received a complaint about Rich Brown and asked if he had witnessed or was aware of any situation about Rich and inappropriate conduct. He told Joe and me that he had lunch with Kathy on Tuesday of last week. He said that she said that Rich was making her feel uncomfortable and that she wanted to talk about reapplying for the position in Accounting. Bob said he just talked to her as a friend. I asked Bob if there was anything else he wanted to tell us. He said no. I thanked him for speaking with us and asked him to keep our conversation confidential.

RESOLUTION:

There had been prior incidents many years ago, which were dealt with by verbal/written reprimands. Many of the complaints seem more like personality conflicts as to management style (e.g., questions about her name, where she was going, etc.) The other events do not appear to be severe or pervasive in the workforce but should still be addressed with discipline. Rich will be removed from his position and will be offered the option of resigning. He will be demoted until such time as his inappropriate behavior ceases.

The University of Knowledge

This certifies that

Julie Burkhart

has satisfactorily completed

WordPerfect for Beginners

offered by the Office of Community Education
The University of Knowledge

Jay Schmidt

Dean of Community Education

Harassment Policy
(includes retaliation language)

All Forms of Harassment Are Prohibited

The Company values a professional environment where each employee is treated with respect and dignity. The Company expressly prohibits any form of harassment based on sex (with or without sexual conduct), race, color, religion, pregnancy, national origin, age, disability, sexual orientation, or status as a veteran, Vietnam-era or special disabled veteran, or protected activity. The Company also prohibits same-sex harassment.

The Company also recognizes that employees with life-threatening illnesses, including cancer, heart disease, and those employees living with HIV and AIDS, may wish to continue their normal pursuits, including work. As long as these employees can meet performance criteria and their conditions do not pose a threat to themselves or to others, they will be treated consistently with other employees. Interference with the ability of employees to perform job duties is not tolerated. Any employee refusing to work with an employee with a disability or a communicable disease, after receiving information concerning the disability or disease, may be subject to discipline, including termination. Harassment of employees with disabilities or with communicable diseases will not be tolerated.

In order to create a productive work environment free of bias, it is the Company's policy that conduct by any employee that harasses, disrupts or interferes with another employee's work performance, or that creates an intimidating, offensive or hostile work environment, will not be tolerated. It is important to remember that even humor, when interpreted by another as offensive, may constitute a form of harassment.

This policy applies to workplace conduct, conduct at Company functions or while on Company business, and to employees at all levels and positions within the Company.

Sexual Harassment

It is impossible to list all behaviors that could constitute sexual harassment. Generally, sexual harassment is unwelcome behavior (which may or may not include sexual conduct). Both males and females can be victims of sexual harassment by persons of the same or opposite gender.

Prohibited behaviors that may constitute sexual harassment include:

A. Unwelcome sexual advances, requests for sexual favors, and all other conduct of a sexual or otherwise offensive nature, especially where (1) submission to such conduct is made either explicitly or implicitly a term or condition of employment, (2) submission to or rejection of such conduct is used or threatened to be used as the basis for decisions affecting an individual's employment, or (3) such conduct has the purpose or effect of unreasonably interfering with an individual's work performance or creating an intimidating, hostile or offensive working environment.

B. Verbal abuse, offensive gestures or leering, sexually degrading words, offensive comments, jokes, innuendoes, sexual content added to work-related conversations, and other sexually oriented statements.

C. Graphic, degrading, condescending, or suggestive comments about an individual's body.

D. Unwanted flirtations, propositions, or physical contact or any threats of undesired contact. Repeated invitations when the recipient has indicated that he or she is not interested.

E. Improper questions about an employee's private life.

F. Circulating, displaying, downloading, viewing or disseminating material (electronically or otherwise) that ridicules a gender or is obscene, inappropriate, offensive, degrading, sexually suggestive or explicit, regardless of whether it is directed at specific individuals.

G. Retaliation against an employee for truthfully complaining about or reporting prohibited behaviors.

Harassment Complaint Procedure

Employees are expected to treat co-workers with respect and to refrain from any conduct that may be construed as harassment. If you experience or observe any job-related harassment by employees, customers, or other third-parties based on sex, race, or any other factor, or if you believe that you have been treated in an unlawful, discriminatory manner, it is your duty to promptly report the incident to your human resources department. You are not required to complain first to the person who is harassing you. If for any reason you are not comfortable reporting the incident to the human resources department, then you should bring the situation to the attention of any senior officer, including the President. Your complaint will be kept confidential to the extent possible, as determined by the Company. While your initial complaint may be made verbally, the Company may request a written statement of your complaint to facilitate the investigation of your complaint.

All employees are expected to cooperate in investigations of harassment complaints by providing truthful information in response to any inquiry. The Company prohibits any form of retaliation against any employee for filing a truthful complaint under this policy or for assisting in a complaint investigation. Retaliation may result in disciplinary action, up to and including termination. However, if after investigating any complaint of harassment the Company should determine that the complaint was untruthful or that an employee has provided false information regarding the complaint, disciplinary action, up to and including termination, may be taken against an individual who knowingly filed an untruthful complaint or gave false information.

The Company will investigate any claims of harassment promptly, impartially, thoroughly and, to the extent possible, confidentially. The manner and extent of investigation is at the discretion of the human resources department as it deems necessary. However, if an employee is not satisfied with the way a complaint or investigation is handled, he or she should bring this to the attention of a senior officer or the President. In all cases, the employee making the complaint will be advised when an investigation has been concluded.

▶ Index